More Praise for *Birds of a Feather*

"Surprising and deeply moving. This is the true story of one woman's quest to help individuals who have suffered great trauma . . ."

—INGRID NEWKIRK, founder/president, People for
the Ethical Treatment of Animals (PETA)

"Inspiring and heartwarming. Dr. Lindner's story gives us hope for the future."

—BOB BARKER

"A magical story. Dr. Lindner reminds us to be open to the possibility that healing sometimes comes in unexpected forms."

—ROBERT KENNER, director of *Food, Inc.*, and
Merchants of Doubt, and *Birds of a Feather*

"Lindner's book poignantly entwines three narratives: stories of humans ravaged by their experiences of war, stories of parrots (and later canids) ravaged by maltreatment, and her own story—how she finds a way to help these humans and nonhumans simultaneously *and* synergistically."

—IRENE M. PEPPERBERG, PhD; research associate,
Harvard University, author of the
New York Times bestseller *Alex & Me*

"I wish this book had been available to me when I was first trying to learn the ways of parrots. My life was likewise turned around by the birds, who ended up getting me off the street. *Birds of a Feather* is both well written and engaging . . ."

—MARK BITTNER, author of the *New York Times*
bestseller *The Wild Parrots of Telegraph Hill*

"The real-life stories in this book will touch your heart and make you look at the world in a different way."

—PATTY SHENKER, president of the Animal Acres
Sanctuary and Dream Catcher Sanctuary

"Lindner has been a champion for all animals, but she always held a special place in her heart for birds. It's a love beyond measure and with a keen understanding of their complex emotions, superior intelligence, and needs."

—VERNON WEIR, director,
American Sanctuary Association

"Through the tears of sadness, and hope, I congratulate Lorin Lindner on her wonderful writing about the *Birds of a Feather.*"

—TIPPI HEDREN, president, the Roar Foundation,
the Shambala Preserve

"This heartfelt book demonstrates that kindness to animals is also good for people, and that caring for others helps to heal ourselves."

—GENE BAUR, cofounder and president of Farm
Sanctuary and author of *Farm Sanctuary*

"Dr. Lindner has conjured up a magical sanctuary where the weathered and the feathered find mutual serenity."

—KEVIN MCKEOWN, former mayor,
Santa Monica, California

"A sweet story with a profound message! It is a story with heart and sensibility."

—THEODORA CAPALDO, ED.D., president emeritus,
New England Anti-Vivisection Society

"If only more people extended themselves like Lorin Lindner has—the world would be a much better place."

—JOANNA CASSIDY, actress, *Blade Runner*

"This book demonstrates that there are true healers in the world—and we could use more people like them."

—MICHAEL BELL, actor, voice animator, and director

"This is the story of how love, ambition, and hope can succeed beyond our wildest dreams."

—ALAN STEWART, DVM, DACVIM,
veterinarian, playwright

Birds of a Feather

Birds of a Feather

A True Story of

Hope and the Healing

Power

of Animals

Lorin Lindner

with Elizabeth Butler-Witter

St. Martin's Press  New York

BIRDS OF A FEATHER. Copyright © 2018 by Lorin Lindner. All rights reserved. Printed in the United States of America. For information, address St. Martin's Press, 175 Fifth Avenue, New York, NY 10010.

Design by Meryl Sussman Levavi

www.stmartins.com

Library of Congress Cataloging-in-Publication Data

Names: Lindner, Lorin, author.
Title: Birds of a feather : a true story of hope and the healing power of animals / Lorin Lindner.
Description: First edition. | New York : St. Martin's Press, 2018.
Identifiers: LCCN 2017055117| ISBN 9781250132635 (hardcover) | ISBN 9781250132642 (ebook)
Subjects: LCSH: Parrots—Therapeutic use—Anecdotes. | Veterans—Mental health. | Post-traumatic stress disorder—Treatment.
Classification: LCC RC489.P47 L56 2018 | DDC 616.89/1658—dc23
LC record available at https://lccn.loc.gov/2017055117

Our books may be purchased in bulk for promotional, educational, or business use. Please contact your local bookseller or the Macmillan Corporate and Premium Sales Department at 1-800-221-7945, extension 5442, or by e-mail at MacmillanSpecialMarkets@macmillan.com.

First Edition: May 2018

10 9 8 7 6 5 4 3 2 1

To my husband, my father, my brother, and all the service members who made sacrifices for our freedom. And to Sammy, Mango, and all the other parrots who made sacrifices of their freedom.

Contents

Birds of a Feather

Prologue

I pulled up to a modest house in South-Central Los Angeles, nearly identical to the others on the street, to collect a Moluccan cockatoo. It was 2007, and I'd been rescuing birds for twenty years. I'd walked into well-kept suburban mansions, sleek high-rises, and crumbling apartment blocks to rescue birds. No matter what the exterior of the buildings looked like, what I found inside was often the same: Birds isolated in lonely cages. Birds who didn't have enough food. Birds living in their own filth. Birds who were abused. It still breaks my heart every time, and the tragedy is that it's all so ordinary. Across the United States and the rest of the world, the scene is repeated thousands of times. With each rescue, though, we end that suffering for at least one bird. Serenity Park, the sanctuary I had just opened, was accepting the parrot—Rascal, the intake paperwork called him—as a surrender. This bird, at least, I told myself, was headed toward a different, better fate.

Toys were scattered across the small lawn. As I walked up to the house, I heard the yells of children playing. I knocked on the door, and the noise stopped.

A woman, with several children gathered behind her, answered. "I'm here to pick up Rascal," I said.

I smiled at the name. Serenity Park had taken in several Moluccan cockatoos, and I knew just what rascals they could be.

"Rascal's not home."

Not home? It's not as if a parrot can go out for a drive.

"Would you like me to come back later?" I asked.

"Nah, you can go on and take the bird. You don't need my husband for that."

So Rascal was the husband. That made sense, too.

"Rascal won Pilot in a poker game," the woman explained, "but we can't do anything with him. He bit two of the kids."

The two eldest children led me to a small, windowless shed in the backyard. When we opened the door, it was hard to see in the dim light. There, among a jumble of lawn equipment and old toys, I could just make out a small cage. Inside, Pilot flapped frantically and began to scream.

Moluccan cockatoos are white-tinged with a faint pink color, and when they lift the large crests on their heads, they reveal darker, salmon-colored feathers. Their feathers are beautiful in the light of the sun, but Pilot was hidden in the dark, dusty shed. Cockatoos are often over a foot and a half long, and Pilot was on the large end. He was a huge, untamed beast of a bird. He blinked repeatedly in response to the bright sun. His cage, much too small for a bird of his size, was made of chicken wire. He had no perch. Parrot feet are made to clutch branches, not stand on flat ground. His toenails were curled up in a tight coil, so he shifted uncomfortably. He screamed, and I could see into his mouth, where small white patches covered his tongue and throat. His beak was enormous and crooked, a condition sometimes found in cockatoos and correctable with veterinary treatment, and he could not close it entirely. I wondered how he could chew. And his nares (bird nostrils) were crusted and plugged.

He screamed again, the metal walls amplifying the sound in a way that must have terrified him. I was not about to ask if the bird was up to date on his vaccinations. I planned to take him straight to Dr. Frank Lavac at the Wilshire Animal Hospital, the veterinarian who examined all the parrots before they came to live at Serenity Park. Pilot would need to be quarantined until his blood test results came back. From the white patches in his mouth, I could see that, at the very least, he had a serious vitamin A deficiency.

"You're going to be okay now, Pilot," I told him as I picked up his cage.

He screamed again and threw himself against the chicken wire, desperate to get away. I spoke quietly, letting him get used to me. I knew he was frightened, but I promised him his life was about to change forever.

* * *

Matt Simmons, the director of operations at Serenity Park, was walking to work one day when he saw a man standing at the Veterans Administration (VA) West Los Angeles Medical

Center shuttle stop. His face was wrinkled from hard living, his fingernails yellowed and cracked. He was wearing a hospital gown and flip-flops. He held his IV pole in one hand as he fumbled to pull a cigarette from a pack with the other.

"Got a light?" the man asked Matt.

"Uh, yeah, but should you be smoking?" Matt asked.

The man shrugged. "They told me I shouldn't leave the hospital either," he said. "But here I am."

Matt handed him a lighter and introduced himself.

"Where did you serve?" Matt asked him, thinking he might say Vietnam.

"Iraq," he said. "The first one, Desert Storm." Matt had fought in the same war.

The man said his name was Smitty, and he had been a Seabee in the navy. His team went in before the full deployment of soldiers and sailors to lay down roads and runways. A team like that can turn a desert into a fully operative city in a matter of days. Matt had always admired the Seabees. They built the infrastructure that had allowed him to land in relative comfort.

"Where ya heading?" Matt asked.

"I figure my ex-wife will let me sleep in the garage." She was good that way, Smitty said, even though she didn't like his drinking, and she didn't like their children finding him passed out.

His hands shook as he tried to light his cigarette. They always shook when he went without a drink for more than a few hours. One morning, the shaking got so bad that Smitty chipped his tooth on a whiskey bottle, so he started pouring his liquor into plastic containers. Two days ago, when his children tried to wake him, he didn't respond. The ambulance brought him to the VA. The detox staff was worried he'd develop seizures from withdrawal, and they urged him to stay. But Smitty was going to leave, whether they checked him out or not.

Until he met Matt.

I'm not sure what Matt said, but he convinced Smitty to follow him back to New Directions, a program on the VA grounds that helps homeless veterans addicted to drugs and alcohol. Maybe just speaking with a fellow veteran helped Smitty. Maybe he realized he was shaking, nearly undressed, at a bus stop, and needed help.

"It takes about a week to adjust," Matt told Smitty, "so don't think about leaving until you give it some time."

Although he was an addict himself, Smitty didn't like illegal-drug users. Drinking, he thought, was legal. Drinking didn't make people steal from their families or go away to prison. He had a hard time adjusting to New Directions, where alcoholics were in the minority. Most men in the program were homeless veterans addicted to heroin, prescription opioids, or anything that dulled their pain.

Matt was afraid Smitty would feel trapped among so many drug users, so once Smitty finished his daily work at New Directions, where he was up before dawn for exercise, manual labor, and therapy, Matt began bringing him to work at Serenity Park. The place isn't just a parrot sanctuary, after all; it is a veterans' sanctuary, too. I founded it on the grounds of the VA as a place where wounded warriors and wounded parrots could work toward healing together.

Smitty didn't get it, at least at first. He didn't understand how working with parrots could help him. Still, he liked the physical labor. He used the skills he'd learned as a Seabee to help lay foundations for new aviaries, clear a space for a new kitchen, and trench rows for flower beds. He didn't talk much, but he worked all day. He was exhausted each night, and that meant that for the first time in years he got a good night's sleep without alcohol or sleeping meds.

Matt encouraged Smitty to work the Twelve Steps of Alcoholics Anonymous. As a recovering addict himself, Matt knew that talking honestly about alcoholism was difficult for many veterans, so he asked Smitty to start with something else.

"Try something a little weird," he said. "Tell your story to one of the parrots."

"I don't think so," Smitty muttered.

Pilot had recently arrived at Serenity Park. Cockatoos have powerful beaks and sharp nails, and we knew he'd bitten people, so he was in an enclosure by himself. When he was scared, as he often was in those first weeks, he would open his mouth wide, threatening to bite. He extended his crest and his wings, making himself look large and menacing. Most of the time, he huddled in his privacy box, a space we give to each parrot where they feel safe and hidden.

I told the veterans to be careful around Pilot. He had experienced severe trauma, and I didn't know how he'd react to humans. "Clean his aviary, give him his food, then get out," I said.

Smitty was quiet, so he was often assigned to the duties in and around Pilot's aviary. He'd do his work, just as I asked, and leave Pilot alone. Pilot watched him warily, quick to scream or puff out his chest. Smitty didn't react. It was almost as if he didn't notice Pilot at all. After a few weeks, Pilot began coming out of his box when Smitty arrived. He stopped screaming. Instead, he cocked his head and watched Smitty work.

At least Pilot is healing, I thought.

Then one day, when he was working in Pilot's enclosure, I heard Smitty whispering to someone: "You won't tell, will you, boy? My secret will be safe with you."

Smitty never saw direct combat, though he saw plenty of body bags on the transport helicopters bringing guys back to base. A worse trauma came after the war, when he and his brother were driving on the Pacific Coast Highway. Smitty was sober, but his brother was high. "Faster," his brother urged Smitty. "Go faster." When Smitty rounded a curve at eighty miles per hour, he lost control, and they broke through the guardrails and tumbled more than one hundred feet down a cliff. Smitty broke both femurs, his collarbone, some ribs, and his neck. His brother was thrown from the car and died. His mother never forgave him. He never forgave himself.

Smitty began drinking. He lost his job. He stopped spending time with his family. He lost his friends. To the extent he had any life at all, it was spent drinking himself into a stupor on a cot in his ex-wife's garage.

Smitty looked at Pilot. "You know what it's like, don't you, boy," I heard him whisper, "to feel worthless."

Smitty didn't like the talkative or outwardly affectionate parrots, but he spent an hour or more a day with Pilot. At first, Pilot would sit on a perch, close to the safety of his box, while Smitty worked. Eventually, though, he'd let out a call, not of terror, but of welcome, when Smitty arrived. He'd fly down, and the two would sit near each other on a chair. Pilot never became a cuddler, and he never sat on Smitty's shoulder as some birds do with their special veterans, but he was a good listener. That's what Smitty needed: to see eye to eye with a creature who shared his pain.

"I can still hear him," Smitty said, "telling me to go faster. Why did I listen, Pilot? Why did I have to be the one to live?"

Sharing that story, and admitting that his alcohol use was out of control, turned out to be the first step in moving forward, the first step in changing the narrative of guilt and shame that played in Smitty's head. His journey to healing wasn't going to be quick or easy, but at least it had begun.

Smitty was one of our best workers, but we all celebrated the day he left Serenity Park. He was going home to be with his family, and they would have a second chance together.

"When you told me what Pilot had been through," Smitty said later, "I wondered how he would want to keep living after all that, but you just do; you put one foot in front of the other and make every day a little bit better than the last." He paused, and I don't know if he was talking about Pilot or himself when he said: "Maybe there's a happy ending after all."

ONE

A Promise Is Made

A Robin Red breast in a Cage
Puts all Heaven in a Rage

—WILLIAM BLAKE, "Auguries of Innocence"

On Christmas Eve in 1987, a bird's screams echoed through the canyons of the Beverly Hills neighborhood of Trousdale Estates. The sound was a high-pitched, warbling wail, like a woman in agony, and it went on for hours. In the bird's native land, 8,200 miles away, the cry would enable wild parrots to alert each other through dense rainforest to predators circling in the sky or crouching in the trees. In Trousdale Estates, a neighborhood full of multi-million-dollar homes carefully arranged on the hillsides, the sound reverberated through the otherwise peaceful and empty streets. This was the kind of place where celebrities and millionaires enjoyed the views of Los Angeles from their private pools, not where wild animals screamed for hours.

Neighbors called the police and animal rescue groups.

Animal Control contacted a friend of mine who worked with one of the animal rescue groups. She said she needed to find a foster home quickly, and she knew I loved birds.

"Do you think you can take in a parrot?" she asked. "If we don't move right away, Animal Control will take it. We need help tonight."

I was in the middle of studying for the Psychology Licensing Exam. Our professors warned us not to take on any additional responsibilities, and they told dire stories about low pass rates. This wasn't the time for weddings, pregnancies, or new jobs. It was Christmas Eve, though. Everyone else was going to take a break. I could help, I thought.

"I'll keep it until we can find it a good home," I said.

When we arrived that evening, Animal Control officers escorted us into the mansion. It was for sale, unfurnished, and our footsteps echoed through the empty rooms. The house spread out from an airy central atrium. The walls were painted a light peach, and tall potted palms decorated the space. In a cage at the center of the atrium was a single Moluccan cockatoo. Nearly two feet long, she had pink feathers, and when she raised her crest, it was a rich salmon color. Her colors complemented the cool pastels and whites of the home. The owners thought the bird's beauty would help them sell the house quickly.

For the bird, there was nothing beautiful about the space. There were no toys, no mirror or bell, nothing to stimulate and entertain her. No fruit or vegetables to pique her interest. No voices, bird or human, to comfort her. She was utterly alone. Her droppings had piled up like a pyramid to perch level.

Her cage had several locks, and she'd managed to open

most of them. She couldn't get out, but I could see there was an intelligent mind trapped in that cage.

My heart quickened when I saw the seed bowl full of empty hulls. I examined her keel, the breastbone that typically gets fattened up in chickens, and saw the sharp bone protruding from her chest. She didn't have an ounce of fat. When Animal Control contacted the owners, they claimed they were sending their chauffeur about once a week to replenish her seed bowl. It is tragically easy to starve a parrot to death, because they eat only the insides of seeds, leaving the nutritionally valueless hulls behind. To the untrained eye, such as that of a chauffeur hired to drive a car, it can appear as though the seed bowl is still full when only empty hulls remain.

I'd seen people make this mistake before with parrots. One woman told me she had asked her children to feed her bird while she was away. She called daily to remind them to check his food. "Don't worry. His bowl is full!" the children told her. That bird died an appalling death, even with people to care for him. Now I was seeing another animal who had been abandoned and starved, even while surrounded by vast wealth.

I looked from her keel to her eyes. There was fear there; she didn't understand that we were there to help. There was also hope. Maybe, at last, someone had come to keep her company and rescue her. Mostly, though, I saw pain. I felt as if I were looking directly into a tortured soul. Those eyes seemed to be crying out to me.

I can't explain it. I felt an immediate bond with this bird. I knew then that this rescue was going to take more than a few hours.

"I promise," I said, "to find you a good home. I promise to make you happy."

But what makes a parrot happy? Far too few pet owners know the answer to that question. Owning a bird is seductive, but people often don't consider the difficulties of keeping an exotic animal. They want to care for and love a beautiful creature, but unless they understand the commitment involved, they can end up doing more harm than good.

I knew the damage humans could inflict, but still, I could relate to wanting a bird. I always enjoyed being in their presence, but I had vowed years ago not to be a part of the animal trade. Here, though, was an animal not in a pet shop but left alone in a house for sale, because she complemented the decor. Here was an animal who needed me.

And this parrot was not your average pet—not just because she had the intelligence to pick locks. Her pink feathers were the color I'd painted my bedroom as a child. I wasn't immune to the seduction of a parrot's beauty. She was tall with a broad chest. Her large black eyes were surrounded by circles of blue. And she was hungry and afraid.

I realized I needed to learn what it would take to do right by this bird. She had never asked to be brought to this hemisphere, this continent. She had not asked to be isolated in a human world. I promised her she would have a permanent home.

I took her in. I gave her a human name, Sammy, short for Salmon, in honor of her beautiful salmon-colored crest. I had to learn how to provide the care she needed. And what I discovered ended up helping many others, parrot and human alike. Though I had no way of knowing it at the time, Sammy would lead me to a career of helping veterans find their way to healing. She wouldn't be a distraction from my Psychology Licensing Exam; she would utterly change my views about my profession. And, perhaps most of all, Sammy would help me find my way to a life of love and service.

* * *

I wanted to understand where this bird had come from. I felt that if I knew her history, I'd know better how to care for her now. So I researched Sammy's roots. I wasn't there when Sammy was a baby, but I can imagine her early life because it's the story of millions of birds wrenched from their homes in the wild.

With a likely birth year of 1977, based on the date of her importation, Sammy was wild-caught as a fledgling in the Moluccas, a mountainous Indonesian archipelago made up of over a thousand islands. Most are covered with rainforest or plantations heavy with the scents of clove and nutmeg. The archipelago teems with abundant and often unique animal life: nocturnal marsupials, civets, wild pigs, and hundreds of species of birds, including the Moluccan cockatoo. While her parents guarded her and searched their island for food, little Sammy was sheltered in the safety of their nest, a hollow in a tree lined with leaves and sticks to cradle her. The nest was fifteen to a hundred feet from the ground, a snug and carefully constructed sanctuary.

On the day she was captured, Sammy awoke nestled next to her brother. She was just a baby. She felt warm, comfortable, and only half-awake. It was mostly dark in the nest, a space just large enough for the young birds and their parents to snuggle together. The light that filtered through the twigs and the small opening was tinged with green from the thick forest canopy. It was early, but the air was already moist and warm. The sounds of the rainforest were muffled by the nest, but she could still make out the chattering of the forest animals. Most of Sammy's feathers had come out of their hard sheaths, and she was soft and fuzzy. So was her brother.

Baby cockatoos in the wild generally do not leave their nests until they are about twelve weeks old, so this small space was the only world Sammy had ever known.

When she'd first opened her eyes, weeks ago, she'd seen her mother and father, and she'd felt immediate comfort and calm. This feeling is a result of imprinting, though Sammy didn't know that. She just knew she trusted this constant presence in her life: feeding her, grooming her, warming her when night came. She had grown in her parents' care from a tiny, featherless, sightless hatchling into a strong young bird.

Her brother lay by her side, her parents brought food, and when she awoke each morning to the chatter of her flock, her body felt a little stronger. Soon she'd step outside and spread her wings for the first time. She'd hop from branch to branch, watching and learning from her flock, stretching her boundaries until, with practice, she, too, would begin to fly. When she could keep up with the flock, her parents would wean her, and she'd fly for miles searching for nuts, roots, and fruit.

Her immediate family was part of a larger flock. The calls of her flockmates near the nest were familiar. Their sounds meant safety. Development threatens many of the natural areas in the islands, but Sammy didn't know about the changes going on around her. She was far from the ground and its worries.

This day, though, something was wrong. She was hungry, and her parents were gone. Her father hadn't come back from foraging. There was no one to chew up seeds of fruit and carefully feed them to her. Her mother, who had been near her every moment she'd been conscious, had left as well.

She heard a horrible screech near the nest, sharp and loud to begin with, then weakening to a wail. Sammy was accustomed to cries warning of predators in the air or on the ground. This sound was different, a shriek of pure pain followed by despair. It sounded like Sammy's older sister. Why was her sister screaming like that? What was happening? Sammy crept toward the back of the nest. An uncontrollable shaking spread through her body. She shuddered.

The noise Sammy heard was the sound of a flockmate being fastened to a tree. When hunters take parrots from the wild, the first step is often securing a fledgling to a tree branch, either with rope or, to make the cries even louder, with nails. The tiny bird's distress call can be heard for miles around, drawing in her flockmates. The hunters count on the flock gathering together in one place, making the parrots easier to capture.

Sammy heard a mad cacophony near the nest; whatever had caused the first outcry was not going away. When Moluccan cockatoos notice a flockmate in trouble, they rush to the sound. The flock gathers together to deter predators. Their best defense is as a group.

Hunters and poachers commonly cut down trees with nests, blighting the forest. Sammy felt a rumbling, and the nest, the entire tree, began to shake. She had never experienced anything like it. To her, the nest meant safety, comfort, family. It swayed only when the wind and rain shook the tree. How could it be moving like this, as if the entire earth were trembling? The air was filled with a thick, unnatural stench, and tendrils of black smoke from a big machine made their way into the nest. She huddled, tucked her head, and shut her eyes.

Then came the sickening fall. Time seemed to stop as she felt her home crash down. The boom shook the forest.

After the flock came to the rescue, hunters threw a net over the birds. If the parents are present—and they usually are, as Moluccan cockatoos commonly mate for life and raise offspring together—poachers capture them, too. Adult parrots can be quite fierce; their beaks can exert a force of five hundred pounds per square inch and they will fight sometimes to the death for their babies.

Sammy heard dozens of parrots screaming, but she couldn't tell them apart in the chaos. The nest had broken open in the fall, and the bright light, Sammy's first view of the open sky, blinded her. She tried to crawl under the nest. She cried for her parents, but no birds flew to her.

Something pulled her from her nest, a strong, foreign grip. Sammy thrashed and bit but couldn't free herself from the grasp. She tumbled into an enclosure. She couldn't see in the darkness. Her flockmates were all around her, packed tightly together. But there was no comfort here. Most of the birds screamed, but some were quiet. Some didn't move at all.

Where were her parents? Where were her brother and sister? Sammy shook and cried out. She felt something placed inside her beak and very soon afterward her body grew heavy, her eyes closed. Sammy lost consciousness and didn't feel anything else for a long time.

She was now part of the wild-bird trade.

* * *

Over 50 percent of birds caught in the wild will die during either their capture or transport to market. Importers care little about the lives lost, as long as their profits remain high. Dead birds are an acceptable cost of doing business.

As in many exchanges between the West and the developing world, wealthy countries benefit far more from the trade than poor ones. Local areas suffer deforestation and loss of native species. A small fraction of the money made from the trade goes to the locals; most ends up in the hands of westerners. Once the trees and wildlife are gone, the locals no longer have a source of income.

The captured birds are kept in tiny cages in the marketplaces of cities such as Ambon and Jakarta. Conditions vary, but it's not unusual for the birds to be left in unshaded boxes without food or water. The cages are rarely cleaned, leading to the spread of disease among birds already weakened by the rigors of capture and transport. Wildlife traders, often tied to the worldwide drug and weapons trades, purchase the birds in the market. Drugs, weapons, and wildlife are among the top criminal trades on the planet, and the skills and criminal networks needed for one type of illegal smuggling are easily employed in another. The crucial difference is that animals are living, unwilling participants.

To keep the birds quiet during shipment—typically to the United States and Europe—smugglers use drugs and/or restraints. Thankfully, bringing wild-caught birds into the United States became illegal in the 1980s and in Europe it became illegal in 2006, but, regrettably, that ban never entirely stopped this highly lucrative trade. Crammed into poorly ventilated suitcases or stuffed into pipes to keep them hidden, innumerable birds die during shipment. They succumb to heat, crowding, hunger, and lack of air. They also die from the vodka forced down their throats to keep them sedated or from the curare intended to keep them immobile.

An American, whom I will call Robert Barnes, was the most notorious exotic-animal trader during the time Sammy was imported to the United States. When he was not traversing the Southern Hemisphere furthering the bird trade, Robert Barnes lived in Los Angeles. He offered ten times a typical annual salary to indigenous people for the safe capture of native birds. To people struggling to feed their families, the money was probably inducement enough, but he also offered baseless promises of a fabulous future for these animals in America. Locals were aware of the effects of habitat loss and deforestation, and they often thought they'd be helping the birds by sending them away.

One great hope for the future of wild birds is that these very same poachers, those people who are trying to make a living to support their families, are now being taught how to use their skills to create an ecotourism industry in their native lands. Former poachers are now becoming experts on parrot behavior. Organizations like the Indonesian Parrot Project, Wild Planet Adventures, and the World Parrot Trust are helping local people build an economy based on protecting their native wildlife instead of capturing and selling it. Now, instead of climbing trees to poach parrot nests, native people are climbing them to build blinds and pulley systems to hoist tourists high into the tree canopy to see the species endemic to those areas. Maybe such a program could have saved Sammy.

When Robert Barnes was importing birds, a legal trade at the time, the next step after transport was entering a quarantine station. Today, quarantine still exists for those birds imported legally or seized during customs inspections. Of those parrots who survive both capture and transport, 25 percent die while in quarantine facilities. Quarantine is designed so that if an animal has a disease it will be detected during the thirty-day hold period. The animals are placed in relatively small, closed boxes. Unlike conventional cages, which at least allow in sound and air, these boxes are meant to completely cut off the parrots, and potential contagions, from the rest of the holding facility. The concern is the spread of disease within the facility and out into the general population; the comfort and safety of individual birds are secondary. Even food and water come in through special openings, not by hand, to prevent the escape of pathogens. These conditions mean the parrots receive no stimulation and certainly no comfort during the quarantine period. It's hardly a way for already weakened social animals to regain their health.

After leaving quarantine, a bird's chances of finding a safe, permanent place to live are not great. Of the 30 to 60 million parrots in captivity (no one knows the exact number), very few find their way to a forever home. I have met many dedicated, loving people capable of providing a comfortable life for the parrots in their care. They number in the hundreds, and I'm certain there are thousands more, but are there millions? Untrained bird owners usually mean well, but many aren't prepared for the work and attention they must devote to their pets. Parrots aren't domesticated animals, so being neat, tidy, and quiet isn't in their nature. As flock animals, they need companionship—more companionship than busy families can usually give.

Even if parrots find satisfactory homes, those homes are rarely permanent. Once people discover what owning a parrot entails, they often pass their bird on to another owner. In addition, people's lives change, and sometimes they may no longer be able to adequately care for their birds, or their birds might outlive them. Longevity is species-dependent, but can be as much as sixty to ninety years in some species, like cockatoos.

We don't treat other domestic animals in the same way. We would never expect dogs or cats to have ten to twenty homes in their lifetimes. One thing that invariably can bring people to tears—I know I cry when I hear such stories—is when an older dog or cat is dumped at the shelter after living all his life with one family. "He's making a mess too often in the house now," the owners say, and the shelter worker nods with coached sympathy. The dog's eyes are full of dissipating hope and mounting fear as the family retreats to its car. I have worked alongside many of these shelter personnel while doing rescue work, and they have told me they long to cry out, "He is part of your family. What are you thinking?" Tens of thousands of elderly companion animals are destroyed each year at shelters after their humans abandon them.

Unlike those elderly dogs, who usually lose their families only once, parrots, with their long life spans, may experience this wrenching move multiple times. People aren't as familiar with birds; they just don't understand them in the same way they understand dogs and cats. After all, we've been living with dogs and cats for thousands of years. Many dogs have been bred to be perpetual puppies, needy and loving, with wagging tails. We breed out the assertive, aggressive behaviors as much as possible. Even domestic cats, seemingly more independent, have smaller brains and fewer aggressive behaviors than their wild cousins.

Parrots have agency and act autonomously. Their motivation is to please themselves, not us. Parrots forage for food and discard it on the ground, heedless of carpets and mess. They build elaborate nests (if no other suitable materials are available, they'll destroy the furniture to do so). They call out and stretch their wings in elaborate courtship rituals. Their behaviors may be fascinating to study, but they're foreign to us, and often annoy the people the birds live with. When parrots are rehomed, most people don't cry; they think someone is just passing on a loud, annoying creature.

Sammy was a survivor. She made it through the capture process. She made it through the long journey across the Pacific. She made it through quarantine. If her flock had twenty birds, it's likely five to seven survived. Whether it was because she was young, had a greater determination to live, or was genetically stronger, somehow, against the odds, she made it. She wouldn't be so lucky when it came to finding a forever home.

I discovered from my research that Robert Barnes, the notorious trader, picked up Sammy after she made it out of quarantine. He sold her to an eighty-year-old woman for five thousand dollars. Given that Sammy was young and could potentially live another seventy years, an elderly person hardly seems like a good fit.

Young Sammy learned to speak like an elderly woman, and for the rest of her life her voice carried the tremulous quality of an older person's speech. When she yelled, "C'mere," she sounded like a grandmother trying to lure a reluctant child into a big hug. Language theorists describe early critical periods for the development of language, and when Sammy learned to speak from her first owner, she was young enough to be the developmental equivalent of a human child learning her first language.

Parrots actively use language to express themselves, much as humans do, and they have a well-developed communication system. So when parrots learn human words they reuse them in context, similar to how chimpanzees and gorillas who have been taught American Sign Language employ human words. Both birds and primates create resourceful combinations to get their points across. "You tickle" is a common phrase across species.

I don't know what kind of home Sammy had with that elderly woman. I hope it was a nurturing one. But, inevitably, upon her owner's death, Sammy went to live with a new person, this time a police officer. He might have been the one to teach her to say "C'mere, give me a beer," though I'll never know. Sammy was with him only one year before the officer committed suicide. Although I have no idea what kind of life Sammy had with this man, I do know he made no provision for the bird or for the scores of fish found in a large tank in his deserted house. As is often the case when owners die, no family member wanted the responsibility of a bird. Sammy ended up back with Robert Barnes, because of the leg-band registration from quarantine. He was perfectly willing to pick her up and sell her to someone else.

Sammy was about nine years old when she reached her next home in Pacific Palisades, the tony coastal town near Los Angeles. The couple who bought her were friends of Barnes and saw her as an opportunity for breeding; a manageable female Moluccan cockatoo can bring in tens of thousands of dollars annually just by laying two clutches of eggs a year, typically two eggs to a clutch. This was not a "birdie mill," a place where, as in puppy mills, the miserable conditions too often produce birds who are sick and weak and who die soon after being brought home. This was a clean home overlooking the ocean. But the back room was stacked from floor to ceiling with cages. Birds of all ages lived packed together: mature breeders, hatchlings, weanlings, and fledglings. A feathered gold mine.

Sammy didn't go the route of becoming a breeding hen, the term for any female bird. Instead, she came into my life because a family in Beverly Hills took a vacation to Hawaii. In many warm places around the world, sidewalk vendors place parrots on tourists' shoulders, then snap a photo of the laughter, and maybe the fear, that follows. I have observed this practice many times on trips to Hawaii and Key West. Tourists see the beautiful parrots, but they don't understand how those birds suffer in the heat day after day, and they don't know that the birds often aren't fed until late at night to prevent them from defecating on tourists' shoulders. The tourists fall in love with the birds, or at least the image they have of them from that family trip. The children (or husband, in the case of the family from Beverly Hills) beg for a bird when they get home, and the family gets a pet. This particular family approached the small-time breeders in Pacific Palisades, and that's where they met Sammy. That captivating bird was just the touch their home needed. She even matched the furniture! They had no idea what they were getting into. They didn't know their adorable pink bird came complete with the messiness, loudness, and destructiveness of a wild animal.

The breeders wanted to keep Sammy for the income she could bring in, and initially refused to sell her. The family raised their offer. The breeders knew Sammy would be a source of money for years and refused again. Finally, the family offered enough money that the breeders gave in. Sammy was sold to her second-to-last home. She lived there a little less than a year. I saw her living situation firsthand when Sammy called out to me on that Christmas Eve, and it was no place for a social, clever, sentient being.

Until she came to live with me, Sammy had been without a flock, lonely, flightless, and essentially in solitary confinement. For ten years, she had suffered.

I had just finished graduate school, and I hadn't even started my practice. I had promised myself no pets while I was still living a student's lifestyle. But I felt a strong bond with Sammy.

I said I would find her a good home; I just didn't realize it would be mine. I couldn't change Sammy's past, but I could make sure the rest of her life was happy. "Don't worry, baby," I said, stroking her feathers. "From now on, everything is going to be okay."

TWO

Penance for Melody

If I can ease one life the aching,
Or cool one pain
Or help one fainting robin
Unto his nest again
I shall not live in vain.

—EMILY DICKINSON, "If I Can Stop
One Heart from Breaking"

Why was I instantly drawn to Sammy? Why would I take time from my studies to take in a bird I'd just chanced upon? Could it possibly be just the moment when our eyes met and I knew her pain? I love animals. I always have. But there was something more that pulled me in and made me want to ease Sammy's suffering.

Perhaps a better question is: How long does guilt last? Was my devotion to Sammy some self-imposed penance for having failed a parrot as a child? Was the guilt still eating away at me for not understanding what that little bird needed?

During my childhood, my mother was often ill and sometimes hospitalized. My father was good-natured and doting, but he just worked too many hours of the day. We moved sixteen times in sixteen years, so it was difficult to find a network to support me. My much-older sister stepped in. She let me talk to her about what I learned in kindergarten. We took long walks together and found animals in the shapes of the clouds. She made sure I ate my dinner and wore my scarf in the snow. When I was seven, though, my sister married and left the city. She got pregnant and had children of her own. I saw her on school breaks, but for much of the time I was lonely.

We had pets, and they were companions and a comfort. There was a dog, kittens, and even once a small alligator. We had Skippy, my sister's green budgerigar, a bird frequently but erroneously called a parakeet. Or maybe "Skippy" should be plural. We went through Skippy I, II, and III; none lived more than a couple of years. I shared a bedroom with my sister, and every night the Skippy of the year would come out of his cage and chat away. He'd offer his running commentary while my sister read from one of the animal stories we both loved. Her birds liked doughnuts dunked in coffee (good thing PETA was not around then, because that could not have been healthy). They were very affectionate birds, and they loved little "butterfly kisses," as my sister called them, a gentle brush with her eyelashes against the sides of their faces. But we had no idea what any of the Skippies needed to live a long, healthy life. In the wild, a budgerigar might live ten to fifteen years or more.

With my sister gone I begged my parents for a parrot—not just a small budgie but a "real" parrot. They agreed. With a sick mother and a busy father, I didn't have enough time with my parents, but I was never short on things. My father would buy almost anything for his "little angel." Looking back, I can see I might have craved that bird as a kind of security blanket. Children usually latch onto a soft cloth object, but the fact that mine was an animal is no surprise.

So here came Melody, a sweet half-moon conure. I remember going to pick her out at the pet store, really just another department in a giant New York City shopping emporium. "That one," I said. She was green, with an orange band over her beak. She was nine or ten inches long, not as large as parrots can be, but much larger than the birds my sister kept, and huge to my seven-year-old eyes. If you looked closely, you could see that her colors changed on different parts of her body, lighter green on the belly, hints of blue near the tips of her wings. When the salesperson brought her out of her cage, Melody was surprisingly soft to the touch, like the downy feathers that escaped from my pillow. She was warm, and she trembled slightly under my fingers. I could feel her heartbeat; it was much faster than mine. I wanted to bring her home, to take away her nervousness, to make her happy.

I loved that little bird. I didn't know how she'd been captured in the wild. I didn't know what she might have suffered on her journey from her native habitat to a store in New York City. I didn't know how much she needed to be with other birds. I didn't understand her need to fly. She was a mystery.

The salesperson, who probably knew more about polyester blends than exotic animals, said that she needed nothing more than a bowlful of birdseed and a little water to keep her happy. We had no reason to question him. Her wings were clipped to keep her from flying, a standard practice at the time and unfortunately common even today, and she had a cage barely wide enough to let her stretch her wings. It was easy, the salesperson assured my family: "A few minutes of work a day, and your bird will practically take care of itself."

We brought her home in our car. It was probably the last time that Melody, a bird who'd evolved to fly huge distances, traveled so far.

I let her out to stroke and pet her, but Melody spent much of her time in a small cage. In our apartment, adults smoked, children wrestled and yelled, my parents laughed and fought. No peaceful sounds of nature, just the din of a young family.

A group of my friends was running through our home one day, and a stray elbow hit her cage. I tried to save Melody, but everything seemed to slow down. The cage wobbled and started to fall. Then, as I ran toward her, everything seemed to speed up again. I was too late. The cage crashed to the floor. She fluttered in panic. She threw herself against the bars. Nowhere to go. No way to escape. When I picked up the cage and set it right, she was still flapping her wings frantically.

No one was intentionally cruel to Melody, and I loved her, but a New York City home with active children and their friends can be a stressful place for an animal who's evolved to live in the wild. She was a good-tempered bird. She rarely bit and she wasn't loud. But neither did she call out with joy when I entered the room or bob up and down in her cage with happiness. She seemed to be existing, not living.

Just like millions of other relinquished parrots, Melody went to another home when we once again moved, this time to Florida. I half-heartedly argued with my parents that we should take her, but I knew I wasn't truly providing her with the best care possible. I knew I had failed her. I loved her, but I could see she wasn't happy. Even then I knew that birds should be with other birds, so I agreed that Melody would stay with our neighbors who had some lovebirds and cockatiels. My parents told me she was happy there, but I'll never really know. I hope she was.

For years afterward, I'd visit parrots in pet stores. I often went with my friend Robin. We'd stroke them and hold them, but although I loved being in their presence, I couldn't stand the thought of putting another bird in a cage.

Robin loved the big parrots, especially the brilliant scarlet macaws. When she moved into an apartment during our first year in college, she bought a baby lilac-crowned Amazon. She couldn't quite afford a macaw. He was a delightful bird, with vivid green feathers set off by flashes of red and yellow and, of course, a lilac-colored head. When he turned sideways to look at you, you could see the playfulness and intelligence in his bright eyes. Since he was still a baby, he would desperately follow Robin wherever she went. This was my first real-life experience of what Konrad Lorenz called imprinting—exactly what I was studying in my biology class at the time. Robin was his surrogate mother. He called to her when she entered a room, and called more loudly when she walked away. She named him Pal, and he really was her best friend.

"Who's a pretty baby," she said as she fed him little treats. He had a beak that could easily crush her fingers, but he took the food gently from her hand.

We laughed as Pal destroyed small pieces of wood faster than any wood chipper. We watched him climb rope ladders (or curtains and bookshelves) faster than any sailor. He'd even roll onto his back, like a puppy in the grass. Robin and her Amazon were a flock of two.

They seemed happy. But what happened to the bird during her long hours at work? I wondered if he missed her. Did he cry all day and pluck his feathers in frustration and lone-liness? This wasn't a cat who could curl up and sleep alone in a favorite hiding spot for fifteen to twenty hours a day. This was a social animal who needed to be near his flock. Always.

Robin wasn't worried about Pal. She fed him, cared for him, played with him, showed him affection. Everyone needs to work, she thought. What was important was the time spent together. The bird did seem happy, I had to admit. He didn't exhibit the behaviors, such as feather shredding and aggres-sion, common in mistreated birds. She lavished attention on him when she was home. She gave him toys for when she was away.

Then she had a baby.

Parrots live long lives. If you're an adult when you buy a young parrot, that bird is almost certain to outlive you. Even smaller birds, such as parakeets and lovebirds, can live up to twenty years. Our lives rarely stay the same for that long. People get sick and die. They move to new homes. People with allergies come into their lives. They get divorced. Or, like Robin, they have children.

The baby took all of Robin's time. She fed her bird and cleaned his cage, but there was no more playing. Pal would fly and walk around the apartment, but there was no special time together, and, except for a few moments perched on Robin's shoulder while she fed or rocked the baby, no cuddling.

As the baby grew, he needed a clean floor to play and crawl on. He learned to grasp at things, including pretty col-ored feathers, and parrots are protective. It felt dangerous to Robin to have a wild bird flying near the baby. The bird went into a cage, and he stayed there. The baby would stare at the bird's bright feathers, but he never touched them.

Her bird had imprinted on her, and, like too many parrots, he was pushed aside as life moved along for his human. For any social animal, that's a disaster. This was his flockmate and his friend, and suddenly she had no time for him.

"You need to let him out," I said, "or find another home for him."

She looked at me patronizingly. "He's fine," she said. "He's a bird. He loves me. It's not like I'm doing anything wrong."

Pal still ate, played with his toys, and groomed himself. Robin was never negligent in making sure he had plenty of food and water, and she kept the cage clean. She gave him no attention, though, and the bird spent his days alone. He began to call out. When he did, she'd cover his cage. Many owners isolate their birds this way to keep them quiet. Their birds are relegated to a garage or a basement, but the owners aren't concerned. They believe parrots are small-brained creatures who don't need much attention or stimulation.

Many years later, another friend, Carolyn, bought a double yellow-headed Amazon parrot. Carolyn lived close to neighbors who had a baby, and the bird learned to imitate the baby's cries. Parrot brains evolved to learn communication from their flock, and if there are no parrots around, they'll imitate the sounds they hear, whether it's a baby crying or a man swearing like a sailor. Carolyn's husband didn't like the bird. They had been fighting, and the bird was another subject of contention. She put her bird in a back room to keep her husband happy. The bird wailed like an infant. It's just mimicry, people said, but if you visited that bird, he would hop up and down with excitement and say hello. He never cried when he had a person to interact with. He cried when he was left alone.

Some people think a bird's cries are not an expression of real emotion. Even as a kid I knew those people were wrong. It seemed to me that unless you plan to care for your parrot as a flock member for the rest of its life, the parrot will always be the one who gets his or her heart broken.

The guilt over surrendering Melody still weighs on my heart. When I saw what happened to my friends' birds, I swore not to keep another parrot as a pet. I knew that many people provide stimulating, nurturing environments for their birds, and they arrange for their parrot's care when they are gone. I knew I was too young and too unsettled to give a bird what he or she needed. For the next fifteen years, I didn't have a bird in my home.

Then came Sammy.

Was I trying to make up for Melody? Maybe. Or maybe there was a real connection when my eyes met Sammy's. Either way, I felt a bond with a creature in pain, and I promised I was going to give her the best life possible.

* * *

I had learned a lot about animals in the years after my family gave up Melody, but once I took in Sammy, I needed a crash course to become an expert. I read every book I could find, and I called every expert whose phone number I could get my hands on.

From the moment I saw her in that empty house, I was

determined to understand Sammy. I didn't see her as just a bird.

No, that's wrong. Sammy was "just a bird," but birds are extraordinary.

Parrots are at least as savvy as primates and marine mammals. Although they do not have a multilayered cerebral cortex, a structure scientists once thought was necessary for advanced cognition, they do have a well-developed nidopallium, a brain structure that serves a similar purpose in birds. In addition, although their brains are relatively small, they are far more densely packed with neurons than mammalian brains. In fact, a small parrot brain may contain as many neurons as that of a midsize primate. Calling someone a "birdbrain" is a real compliment.

We have proof of avian intelligence from watching parrots solve problems and use tools. They use pebbles to grind shells until they are small enough to ingest for much-needed calcium, just as humans use large rocks to grind grain. They use sticks or leaves to keep nuts they're cracking from slipping. They will use a twig to scratch their itchy backs. In captivity, birds learn to operate human contraptions (as anyone who has seen a parrot open the latch on a cage will tell you), and they solve puzzles. Unfortunately, we also have proof because neuroscientists cut open and stain sections of birds' brains to study them. What is evident from parrot behavior has now been substantiated by science, though at a cruel price.

There are over three hundred and fifty species of parrots. They range from tiny parakeets to large, brightly colored macaws. Over a hundred varieties, including all eighteen types of macaw, are endangered. Many parrots are losing their habitats to human development or climate change. Poaching remains a threat as well. Some farmers view parrots as crop-destroying pests and actively try to eliminate them.

Birds, including parrots, likely descended from birdlike dinosaurs similar to archaeopteryx, which lived approximately 150 million years ago. Impressions of feathers have been found along with archaeopteryx fossils. When the great Cretaceous extinction occurred 65 million years ago, all dinosaurs didn't truly die off. Some continued to evolve into modern birds. In Richard Dawkins's richly detailed *The Ancestor's Tale: A Pilgrimage to the Dawn of Evolution*, he describes how the dinosaur tyrannosaurus was a "close cousin" of birds and that this relationship is "made secure by recent spectacular finds of feathered dinosaurs in China."

All parrots, regardless of species, have a curved beak, great for cracking seeds (and occasionally fingers), and four zygodactylous toes, two pointing forward, two backward. Parrot toes are designed for picking up food and for climbing. They're strong and surprisingly dexterous. It turns out an animal does not require an opposable thumb to perform delicate tasks. Parrots do the same thing with a different set of tools. How else could Sammy have picked those locks?

In addition to all the parrots in the wild, of course, millions are kept in cages across the world. Some parrots are isolated in dirty, cramped cages and never allowed to stretch their wings to their full extent. As part of my rescue work, I have been called in on many confiscation cases by humane law enforcement officers who remove parrots from homes because of cruelty or neglect. In some instances, we couldn't even liberate the bird from its cage without first cutting away the bars. In several of our rescues, a bird's tail had contorted into a loop around its perch to fit into an impractically small space; this deformity was especially common in macaws. With their two- to three-foot-long tails, these birds especially feel the physical effects of constricted spaces.

I had seen many birds live contentedly, however, when their human companions acknowledged and provided for their natural needs, and I wanted desperately to learn how to give such a life to Sammy.

What I came to realize is that, although they are incredibly diverse, all parrots need the "Four Fs": foraging, flying, flocking, and, um . . . "mating." Wild parrots who have the Four Fs lead healthy, fulfilling lives and have a better chance of being well adjusted in captivity if those needs continue to be satisfied, but that is a real challenge in domestic settings. Parrots whose needs aren't met often cry out, self-mutilate, and become aggressive. Those are often the ones who end up shuffled from home to home.

In the wild, parrots fly vast distances foraging for food. Diets vary between species and habitats: lorikeets prefer nectar and the keas of New Zealand prefer insects. What species have in common is the need to search out their chosen diet. Finding food demands not just a brain with a well-developed memory and extraordinary mapping skills, but also cooperation, as parrots forage together in groups.

Foraging satisfies a need for variety. I learned to create "forage trays" rich in vegetables and some fruit for Sammy to pick through and eat or discard as she wished. I learned to hang the tray in different locations so she'd have to search it out and feel rewarded by the effort. In the wild, birds often take a little nibble and then move on. Those abandoned morsels never go to waste; in fact, they can grow into whole forests. For parrots who live inside, this behavior leads to dirty floors and frustrated humans. With Sammy as my roommate, I'd learn to become handy with a broom and tolerant of a little extra mess.

Foragers crave mental effort as well. Birds in captivity have a food bowl placed in their cage and as a result have a great deal of time on their hands. Foraging can occupy 30 to 50 percent of a wild bird's day. With this natural act absent from a parrot's repertoire, boredom can set in, and with it come related problems: feather shredding and plucking, self-mutilation, pacing, and other stereotypical behaviors, including head banging. Humans in solitary confinement often resort to self-harm; the same is true for intelligent, social birds. Just as humans require conversation or books, time outside of the cell, and exercise, parrots need to keep their brains busy. Rewarding work is an excellent healer for both species. I've tried many games and activities through the years, but there are a few parrots invariably love: piñatas filled with treats, brainteaser boxes to open for a nut, and treats hidden away in nooks and crannies throughout a bird's living area.

Wild birds often must fly great distances to find an adequate food supply, and flying is just as important to a parrot's physical and mental health as foraging. One month, the trees are fruiting in one part of the parrots' environment, but the next, the birds must search a huge area to get sufficient food. Birds evolved with the need to move. In a domestic setting, flying is often impossible. In fact, many pet owners clip their birds' wings to keep them from flying. If the birds can't fly, the owners think, they'll be more likely to sit happily in their cages or will be safer indoors. The reality is that not being able to fly is equivalent to not being able to walk for a human. Birds don't sit contentedly just because we've made them disabled. Sadly, some domestic birds have had their wings so severely clipped they won't ever fly. Even without working wings, though, these birds still travel around by climbing with their beak and feet.

I needed to provide time and space for Sammy to roam. She was missing feathers, so flying might be difficult, but Sammy would be allowed to walk or climb in my home if she wished after she was "potty trained," which is, fortunately, a relatively easy accomplishment for an animal with a well-developed brain.

Flocking is as crucial to birds as socializing is to humans. Parrots never like to be too distant from their flockmates, and when they can't see them, they call to them. These calls reassure each parrot that it is not too far away from its flock, much as we're reassured when we get texts, tweets, or phone calls from our friends and family.

Parrot calls are unique, not merely among different species of parrot but often within the same species. Just as different groups of humans may speak different languages or dialects, a group of parrots may use very different calls than a group of the same species living only a few miles away. Different flocks of parrots may have different calls to signify "predator coming," for instance. If parrots are transferred from one group to another, some parrots, particularly younger ones, may adapt and "speak" with the new calls. Older parrots, however, will stick together with parrots they already know and continue "speaking" their own language. In human society, immigrants form enclaves where parents feel safe and speak the same language, but their children are more likely to learn the local language and blend in with the community outside the enclave. In this way, we are similar to parrots: we are both animals whose childhood tongues are part of who we are.

This need for communication, and the need for companionship, is as deeply engrained in parrots as it is in humans. A child left alone for extended periods, or an adult locked in solitary confinement, will suffer. They may develop a depressive disorder, or worse. The same is true of parrots. Parrots locked in cages all day will call out for companionship. This calling is one of the primary reasons parrots are kept covered or relegated to spare rooms and garages. The constant cries become insufferable.

Some owners think their parrots are just poorly behaved; the reality is they're satisfying their needs with the only means available to them. It is up to us to learn how to communicate with them so they do not have to scream for us. This is basic Psychology 101—behavior modification: reward behavior you want to repeat and withhold rewards in order to extinguish behavior you want to end. I'd give Sammy a treat when she walked across the room to get my attention rather than calling out.

My condo was in a busy part of Los Angeles. I knew I'd have to do a lot of behavior modification if I was going to keep my neighbors happy and Sammy in my home. Just as too-frequent barking is one of the main reasons people give up their dogs to shelters, parrot squawking is a major reason for relinquishment as well. Companionship would help keep Sammy quiet. I couldn't be a parrot, but I could be a companion. I vowed Sammy would never spend lonely days in a huge, echoing house again.

The final "F," "mating," is vital to parrots. Like humans, parrots tend to mate for life. Actually, maybe they aren't so much like humans: birds don't have a 50 percent divorce rate. Parrots bond strongly with their mates. They stay close to them, and when they lose their partner, they mourn, often refusing to mate again.

Even when birds do not breed, they want another bird to be a companion and partner. Parrots evolved ritualistic courtship behaviors that include stretching their wings, first with long, deliberate extensions of one wing, then the same motions with the other. Cages all too often do not have wide enough areas for such magnificent displays.

Pet parrots are rarely allowed a mate. Many people have only one bird living in isolation. Even if a home has more than one bird, the two might not be compatible, just as a human would be unlikely to find a soul mate in someone picked randomly from the street. It makes for a lonely life for birds who evolved to have a companion.

I could provide some companionship for Sammy, but I knew that eventually I'd have to provide another bird—or more—to keep her happy. Parrots belong in a flock. Would there perhaps be some way I could give her that? The idea of a sanctuary began to grow. I didn't realize it would mean building Serenity Park, but the seed was there.

* * *

Reading books and asking dozens of experts about parrots was one thing; sharing my small home with a thoughtful, intelligent, mischievous, and extremely loud exotic bird was another. I lived in Westwood, where my alma mater, UCLA, is located. Everything was exactly as I liked it. I had been on my own most of my life. It could be lonely sometimes, but it was familiar. I kept my soft white carpets neat by removing my shoes as I entered, a habit I'd picked up in Japan while conducting my doctoral research.

I had never intended to share my home with an animal, even though I loved them. I had been an animal activist prior to getting Sammy, but I had deliberately avoided taking on a sentient being for the rest of our mutual lives. I'd made this decision not only because of my experience with Melody but also because I lived in a relatively small home, and had been in school perpetually since I was five. During the summers, I traveled a great deal. It wouldn't have been fair to a companion animal to be left behind so often.

Now I suddenly had an animal, and a demanding one at that. I knew parrots need to roam, so I put Sammy in her cage only to sleep and when I had to leave her for any prolonged periods (rarely more than a few hours). My pristine white carpet was getting grimier by the day. Newspapers, old towels, rearranging the furniture: nothing could protect it from the onslaught of a bird intent on foraging. When Sammy threw bits of cherry randomly about, leaving indelible burgundy splotches, I stopped trying. If a few stains were the cost of making her happy, then I'd just have to live with them.

I said goodbye to intact furniture. Chunks of wood disappeared from tables and chairs, and scratches appeared everywhere. Sammy decided to build a nest, and she did it inside my favorite soft rocker. She pulled out the interior stuffing and some of the carpet. I'd never been very materialistic, but it's still a little disconcerting to watch many of your possessions being ripped apart.

On top of that there was the noise. When I'd first moved

into this condo I could see all the way west to the ocean off Santa Monica. Student housing for UCLA was largely on the north side of Wilshire Boulevard. I was a block south but easily within walking distance of campus. Single-family homes dotted the quiet neighborhood. Then a construction boom hit, and apartment buildings went up on every side of me. A one-hundred-unit building sprang up directly in front of my windows. No more view of the ocean. Now I had substantially more neighbors, and when Sammy went off on one of her screaming jags, many would come out on their balconies to see if they needed to call Child Protective Services. She sounded like someone being abused.

I was giving Sammy freedom to move, activities to keep her mind busy, food to forage for, and companionship, but even after applying all I'd learned in my research about parrots, we hadn't quite settled in together. Or perhaps I should say she hadn't settled into living with me; I adored her. She still cried out, whether I was home or not, and that look of desperation was still in her eyes.

She was an amazing little creature, and I wanted to win her over. I fed her and pampered her and coddled her. She was a picky eater and I shopped for every type of food she might find irresistible. I went to Southeast Asian markets, plentiful in Los Angeles, and tried all the different fruits and veggies. Like a picky toddler, she'd take a bite and throw the rest to the floor, or one day she'd devour bananas and the next she'd turn her face away.

"Come on, baby," I said. "That's a good little bird. Eat for Mama."

I tried heating up some Gerber hot cereal and hand-feeding it to her. She loved it. Soon she had me trained. She wouldn't eat unless I hand-fed her. I served her food this way every day for quite a while after that, not just once a day but twice.

Her eyes lit up when she saw me moving toward the kitchen. I loved knowing that she was enjoying her food. "Good baby," I said. The flesh around her keel bone began to fatten up.

Within a few weeks, Sammy began to call to me excitedly when I walked into the living room, and not just when she was hungry. When I was home, she'd perch on or near me. Her eyes were brighter. She groomed my hair as if I were a member of her flock.

I began taking Sammy, riding on my shoulder, on walks around the neighborhood. She'd find a tree and climb it, using her strong toes and beak to grip the branches. I climbed up after her, though not as gracefully. Even though she could go higher than I could, and onto branches that would never hold the weight of an adult human, she never left me far behind. No matter how high she climbed, she always came back to my shoulder. It was beginning to feel as if we were a family.

I knew she wouldn't get lost or escape, because she couldn't fly very well. She'd sit still, watching the world around her, taking in the sounds and smells of her temporary perch. I wondered what she thought of up there, if it felt like home or if she puzzled over where the rainforest was. I knew she could see more than I could. Parrots have keen eyesight, and they have cones in their eyes that allow them to see ultraviolet light. Their feathers reflect UV rays, and, to other birds, parrots appear more intricately colored than humans can perceive. Many fruits and berries also reflect

UV rays, while green leaves do not. Seeds must beckon beautifully to a parrot's eyes. Sammy saw a more vibrant world than I did.

She never acted aggressively toward me. She bit me only once, a rarity for birds, and that was while I was playing with her and she couldn't see my hand. Though I don't want to anthropomorphize, she looked aghast and guilty. She showed remorse by immediately putting her head in my hand and clucking. "I didn't mean it," the cluck seemed to say. Sammy and I spent a lot of time playing together. It was more entertaining than anything on television. In fact, I even stopped bothering to turn mine on.

One of her favorite games was hide-and-seek. Usually I would start by saying "Sammy, find Mommy." She knew the chase was on. She would scurry down from her cage and look all over the house for me. The cutest thing was how she would look under the couch. I'm small, but I'm not that small. Or I would chase her, and she would hide under the footstool with her entire tail sticking out. She understood the idea of hiding, but the details were a little fuzzy.

We can never really understand the mind of another animal, but Sammy seemed to be content. She cried out less and less often, though she still made noise. It's natural for even contented birds to call to their flock.

One day, a man in an apartment facing mine came out onto his balcony. He waved and said, "I hear your bird."

Uh-oh, I thought. If one neighbor was annoyed, myriad others must feel the same way.

"We had an aviary at the house when I was a child. I love to hear that sound."

A kindred soul. He was a well-known Persian singer, and

he told me that Sammy reminded him of his home back in Iran. "I can see you like birds as much as I do," he said.

"I think she likes me, too," I said. "She gets so excited when I make her baby food."

"Baby food?"

"It's how I get her to eat. She loves it." I stroked Sammy. "You're Mama's little baby, aren't you?"

He frowned. "She's not a baby. Treating her like a baby will only make her overly dependent."

He was right. I had been doing exactly that. How had I not realized it? When I was a child, I was a picky eater, too, a skinny, gangly kid whom my mother had to entreat to finish any meal. How ironic. Or maybe it wasn't. Maybe I was re-creating a pattern from my childhood. My mother died when I was a teenager, and she'd been sick for years before that. Eating together was one of our bonding activities, too, just like in most families. Even if she didn't eat much herself, she loved finding food to please me. Our family was never the same after my mother died. How could it be?

Now I was taking great pleasure in watching Sammy eat. Her little pupils dilated as she ate something good. I knew which food she was crazy about and how much of it she would eat to the spoonful. I had felt like a mother feeding her adorable child, and I had been feeding that child in myself as well.

Eventually, I gave up feeding her baby food, but the closeness between us remained. I still missed seeing that joy as I fed her, but I realized that hand-feeding her had been as much for me as for her. Birds aren't children. Sammy was a full-grown parrot. I loved her enough to let her be the mature adult she was.

THREE

Mango

After you have exhausted what there is in
business, politics, conviviality, and so on—
have found that none of these finally satisfy, or
permanently wear—what remains? Nature
remains.

—WALT WHITMAN

At first, I'd thought Sammy was a boy. Cockatoos aren't sexually dimorphic; that is, males and females look essentially alike. I had read that the only way to tell the difference is by eye color. Males have dark brown eyes, and females have a lighter brown with a touch of red. Sammy had beautiful, soulful, dark brown eyes. Surely this bird was a male. One day, the slanting light of the waning day was shining right into her eyes, and I saw a bit of red. Had I been wrong? Was my little boy a little girl?

Then Sammy laid an egg.

I had missed the signs that she was ready to lay. There was that nest she'd created inside my favorite plush rocker. She had become acutely attentive to the sounds of other birds on TV and outside in a nearby tree. She'd stare, her body rigid with attention, and listen to what the other birds were saying. She knew that language, even if she didn't speak the dialect. She must have thought me a bit dull for not being as interested as she was. How could I not want to be out there listening all the time?

I started carrying her on more walks around my neighborhood. When we got near a good tree, she'd gesture toward it with her beak. The gesture was just as effective as pointing with a hand or a finger; I had no trouble understanding exactly where she wanted to go. I'd let her climb. One time I looked up and Sammy was fifty feet off the ground. She'd never gone that far before.

"Lady, your bird got away! You'll never get it down," a passerby yelled.

I wasn't afraid. Sammy always came back to me. After giving her some time to survey the sounds and smells of our neighborhood, I held out my arm like a perch, and she deftly climbed back down. People marveled at her fidelity to a human.

Then I noticed she wasn't eating much. After a couple of days, I was worried enough to make an appointment with the veterinarian. However, the appointment wasn't necessary— the veterinarian told me she was about to lay an egg. Sammy wasn't sick, she was busy.

People often believe that birds happily pop out eggs, then move on. They are so used to picking up a dozen at the grocery store that they don't think about the work that goes into them. In reality, laying eggs is difficult. Birds go into labor to produce them, and once they lay them, they are fiercely attached.

The first time it happened, Sammy was sitting in my lap,

and I heard her straining. Then I felt her muscles contracting in regular, rhythmic pulses as she began to push. She leaned back into me as if I were her Lamaze partner. She was panting, working with her entire body. This was no illness, I realized.

Once she was done with the grueling labor, she took a moment to catch her breath and then sat with the egg, keeping it warm. It was oval and whitish, similar to a chicken egg, though smaller. I placed the egg in a large box (I didn't want it to get crushed by someone sitting in the armchair where she'd built her nest), and Sammy climbed in and stayed there. She'd cluck to her egg in the most tender way, and she'd carefully turn it every few hours. She'd come out of the box only a couple of times a day to defecate. She showed less interest in eating than she had before, but I made oatmeal and fed it to her, just as her partner in the wild would have regurgitated food for her to eat. She'd eat a few bites as quickly as she could and run back to check on the egg. She was an excellent mother.

Sammy did not have a partner, so of course her egg was not fertilized. No matter how much care she lavished on it, it would never hatch. After several days, I threw her first egg away, thinking it might rot. Sammy looked into the box. She looked in my chair and underneath it. She was desperate to find it. She moved around my papers and searched in places an egg couldn't possibly fit. Her movements became quicker. She cried out. I had understood that she was attached to her egg, but I'd had no idea how much she'd grieve. The longer she looked, the more frantic her movements became.

Even though I am a vegan, I ran to the 7-Eleven to buy

her a hard-boiled egg. She rejected it, and I decided never to bother her eggs again. She laid several more, and I let her sit on them until she realized they were never going to hatch. Then she would quietly leave the box and not return.

With her increasing interest in the outdoors and her egg-laying, I knew the time had come to find her a partner. I started to ask around the rescue community. Did anyone know of a bird in need of a home?

Then the right bird came to me. I rode my bike to the bank one morning in October of 1988. In the parking lot were three beautiful dogs in a BMW. Alone. With the windows rolled up. I was sweating. Those dogs were in danger.

I yelled into the bank, "Which one of you left your dogs in a BMW?"

A man ran up. "What happened?"

"They're in your car with the windows rolled up. They could die."

He sighed, relieved that his dogs weren't hurt. Then he wrinkled his forehead. "It's not hot," he said, "is it?"

I realized I was warm because I'd been riding my bike. It wasn't really hot. I'd yelled at him for leaving his dogs in the car on a cool October day.

"I love my dogs. I wouldn't hurt them," he said.

He realized I was just trying to protect the dogs, so he wasn't angry. He also cared about animals, he said. Including the cockatoo and the African grey parrot he'd recently bought for his girlfriend.

"What kind of cockatoo?" I immediately asked. When I learned it was a Moluccan and a male, we became quick friends. I asked if his girlfriend would let me bring my bird over for a playdate.

That's when I met Mango.

I knew Sammy couldn't live with just any bird. She needed a bird who was intelligent and playful, who would join in on our games of hide-and-seek. She wasn't a fighter, so she'd need a companion who didn't have an aggressive temperament. Given Sammy's large size, a smaller parrot species would not be suitable for her.

There were many people looking to relinquish other types of cockatoos—sulphur-crested, citrons, and umbrellas. We could have our pick. Ownership of sulphur-crested cockatoos in particular had spiked after the show *Baretta* aired on TV. The star had a darling little cockatoo with a yellow plume as a companion, and he made it look easy—no food being thrown everywhere, no neighbors complaining about screaming, no allergies from the cockatoo dust, no sense of loneliness when the human companion was gone for hours at a time. But that's not the reality, of course. Too many of these long-lived birds were purchased on a whim because of that show and ended up being relinquished again and again, a revolving door of parrots.

Even with all the birds up for adoption, it was hard to find a suitable match. Sammy would have nothing to do with first Mork then Peaches, friends' Moluccan cockatoos, even after several playdates. She stayed near me during our visits, refusing to touch these strange creatures. She wouldn't even look at them.

I was beginning to think maybe we wouldn't find the right match for Sammy, but then we met Mango. As soon as his cage was opened, he crawled up my leg, saying, "Hewwo." He looked at me with one eye as he cocked his head. Cockatoos have peripheral vision, with eyes on either side of their heads, so he needed to turn to get a good look at me.

"Watch out for that one," Barbara, the owner, said. "He bites."

Mango settled into my arms and leaned into my chest.

Barbara shrugged. "I warned you."

Mango didn't bite me. He snuggled into my arms and let me groom him the way Sammy had taught me, gently removing the keratin sheaths from his crest feathers. You have to pinch the cover and pull it off firmly but delicately. Mango seemed to think I had the correct motion.

Mango and Sammy eyed each other carefully. They weren't chatting away and grooming one another, but Sammy wasn't pretending Mango didn't exist. They were making eye contact, sizing one another up.

Sammy and I visited many more times. It wasn't exactly love at first sight—not for Sammy, anyway—but I was falling for Mango. He had an adorable face with a beak twice the size of Sammy's, and he was more white than pink. Though the two birds were the same species, there are many variations. The most noticeable thing was that he had no tail feathers.

"Mango won't fly," Barbara explained. She and her beau had taken him to the park to teach him how to fly as a young bird. "I tossed him up, but he just fell down. He kept breaking his tail. The vet said he couldn't fix it anymore. What kind of bird doesn't want to fly?"

Parrots don't fly just because someone throws them into the air. I wish the vet had explained that fact to Barbara. Birds have to be taught how to take off and use the airstream properly. Wild birds watch their flock members and learn from them, then they begin by flying over short distances. Birds in captivity must have a human to guide them. Birds are timid when they are first learning. Even birds who once knew how to fly will often stop trying once they have had their wings clipped. When they try to take off and those clipped wings make them tumble to the ground, they learn that flying isn't safe.

Sammy had probably never learned to fly, and she was timid about trying. I wanted her to have that gift. She didn't have another bird to observe, so I'd have to teach her. I held her near the bed. "Fly, Sammy, fly," I urged. She was hesitant to leave my arms, but when I let her go, she landed on a soft mattress. With a lot of practice, she began to glide over short distances. Because she was missing so many flight feathers, she'd never go far, but at least she knew the feeling of sailing through the air.

Mango would never fly. Those broken tail feathers ensured that. His owners had no idea what they'd done to him. I learned that Robert Barnes, the same trader who had brought Sammy into the United States, had been the one to sell Mango. Another victim, I thought.

"Anytime you want," I said to Barbara, "I'd love to have Mango stay with us."

It didn't take long before Barbara started asking if Mango could spend the weekends with me. He was biting her so often he was no longer a fun pet, especially when she had parties. I was happy to help. I wanted to be certain she saw me as a resource and that she didn't sell Mango one day without telling me.

Barbara's other bird, Brady, an African grey, stayed home. He was a steel grey with brilliant red tail feathers.

Because Brady was only about a foot long, Barbara could manage him more easily than she could a large cockatoo. He rarely lost his temper and never bit except when Barbara put him to sleep at night. "Don't you ever, ever bite!" she repeated every night as she placed him in his cage. He was very verbal and clever, like many African greys. During the presidential race between George H. W. Bush and Michael Dukakis, Barbara taught him to say "Vote for Bush!" She invited friends over for the last presidential debate. But that night, around the bird's bedtime, as the debate was winding down, the previously silent grey said, "Don't you ever, ever . . . vote for Bush!"

Barbara was not happy.

When Barbara went into the hospital with complications from chronic obstructive pulmonary disease, she asked me to take care of Mango. For the first time, she begged me to take Brady as well. Sadly, she knew she would not be coming home. Unfortunately, before I could pick him up, a neighbor who was watching him left not only the cage door but also the front door open. Brady flew away. I combed the neighborhood and tried everything I'd learned for getting birds back, including playing tapes of African grey and cockatoo voices and leaving an open cage with seeds outside. The neighbor and I searched frantically, posted signs, and called animal shelters, but we never discovered where he went. I hope he found a good home.

Mango was safe with me though. My little family was growing. I didn't realize how lonely it had been until my home was filled with these vivacious personalities. The most important thing was that Sammy had a partner.

There was no need to worry about Mango's intelligence

or sense of humor. At night, he would go into his cage and slam the door repeatedly with his beak until I covered him. He wanted to make sure I knew he had a very strict bedtime. Then he would stick his little leg through the cage bars and switch the lights off. In the morning, he would take the covers off his cage, then Sammy's. He could pick just about any lock, and I never knew if in the morning he would be a free bird or safely ensconced in his cage.

Mango had a toy box on top of his cage. When his behavior was good, he would get a special treat or plaything dropped into the box. A few times a day, he would study the box's contents and make a careful decision. Then he'd pull out his choice, and he'd either tease Sammy, seeming to say "Look what I have! You can't have it!" or he'd try to entice me to play.

One time I couldn't find my gold pen, a special gift I had gotten for graduation. I looked all over—in the bottom of my bag, on the floor, even under the furniture—but it was nowhere to be found. Days later, as I cleaned out Mango's little toy box, I found a stash of my favorite things, including that gold pen. Mango had exquisite taste.

As I was sorting through the box, he watched me closely to see what I might do. Since he had already made deep indentations in the pen with his beak, I decided it was his and left it in the box along with most of the other items he had pilfered from me. He seemed surprised I wasn't mad.

Later that day I learned that a very dear friend had succumbed to AIDS. He had hung on for several months but finally said goodbye and left this world. I wished I could have been there with him at the end, but he was in New York. I would grieve alone. I lay down on my couch and cried.

As I lay there, trying to console myself, I felt something cold on my arm. Mango had carried the gold pen across the room, hauled it up onto the couch, and was now rolling it toward my face with his beak. He made his atoning little clucking sounds all the while.

"No, Mango, Mommy is not sad because of you, precious boy, but thank you for my pen."

* * *

Mango and Sammy got along well enough, but it was clear they'd never form a mated pair. When I sat on the couch, Mango would sit on one end, Sammy on the other. They might be part of my flock, but it was me in the middle, holding us together.

Once they both came to live with me, I realized how much I valued their companionship and their love, but I also knew an ideal place for parrots is one where they are surrounded by similar birds, not in a condo in Los Angeles.

I'd passed the Psychology Licensing Exam, so I'd begun the work I'd spent so much time training for. I'd have to be away from home far more often to be with my clients, and pining for their "flock" all day is no life for parrots.

I'd have to find a solution eventually. What I didn't know was how these two parts of my life would end up so closely intertwined. Sammy and Mango had already brought me joy. I was about to learn from them how birds and humans, both wounded in their own ways, could start healing together.

FOUR

Houseless, Not Homeless

Forgiveness is a virtue of the brave.

—Indira Gandhi

One day sometime in the 1950s, a car drove down a dirt road in rural Alabama. Children crawled over the seats and each other; this was long before seat belts. They had been driving for a long while, and they were getting restless. Their mother, the driver, stared straight in front of her, ignoring the din in the car. She stopped in the middle of the road.

"You go on and get out," the mother said to a little boy in the backseat.

"Why're we getting out here?"

"Just you, Mikey. I need you to get out."

Mikey had never been down this road before. He knew they weren't near their house. He wasn't sure where they were. Mikey looked out the car window. There were no buildings nearby. Nothing but fields and stands of scrub pines.

"Go on now," his mother said.

Mikey got out. His brothers and sisters had quieted down. He couldn't hear anything but the car's engine idling.

"Shut the door," his mother said. Mikey hesitated. He felt panic beginning to crawl inside his chest. But Mikey was used to listening to his elders.

"Mama?" he said.

"Just shut the door," she whispered. She still stared straight ahead. She wouldn't look at him.

Mikey moaned. He wanted to ask why, but he'd been trained not to. He wanted to be a good boy. He swallowed hard, then shut the door.

His mother drove away.

"Wait!" he cried out.

The car sped up. Mikey ran after it, but the car grew smaller.

Mikey's brothers and sisters waved from the rear window.

Mikey kept running until he couldn't see the car anymore, just a thick cloud of red dust.

He heard the insects buzzing. Sweat was running down his face. He wheezed with the heat and the effort and the dust.

He turned in a circle. Nothing. Mikey trembled. He looked around for a car, a house, anything, but he was alone. He couldn't hear the car anymore. A fly buzzed in his ear, but he didn't bother to swat it away.

Mikey sat in the road and cried.

* * *

I opened my private practice in a building just four blocks from my home in Westwood and began seeing clients. It was close enough that I could walk home in the middle of the day to visit Sammy and Mango. They'd call excitedly when I walked in the door, and we'd take a long break playing together. I made sure they were never alone for more than four to five hours at a time.

In the 1980s, dozens of men lived on the streets of Westwood. Los Angeles had fabulous wealth, but it also had people sleeping under tarps and blankets, huddled for warmth. Los Angeles is warm and sunny, but those experiencing homelessness know how quickly the arid climate becomes cold after the sun sets.

For weeks, I saw these men and did nothing, but that felt wrong. I'm a psychologist, I thought. I'm supposed to be helping people. Why should those only be people who have the money to pay me? I couldn't just continue to walk past them as if they didn't exist. Most were mentally ill, addicted to drugs, or both. People didn't end up on the streets because they wanted to be there. They needed help.

A man slept on the sidewalk near my office. "Hey, what's your name?" I asked him one day. He looked startled, as if no one had asked him that in a long time.

His name was Mikey. He "worked" on the same street as I did. "You've got a beautiful face," he'd shout at people passing by. "Let me draw you." He'd make a few dollars from his artwork. He was good at capturing people's faces. He had the biggest smile I ever saw, and it began in his heart. Approaching him was easy.

Mikey could talk. He was that one guy in the neighborhood who seemed to know everybody and who passed on all the news. His life was hardly comfortable, but he was always laughing.

Mikey's life wasn't easy after his mother left him on that

road. It was probably difficult even before that abandonment. Another family took him in, but his new siblings never accepted him. He was an outcast. But Mikey is intelligent, and as soon as he could, he found a way out by enlisting in the military. That was no escape. He served during the Vietnam War, and he experienced its horrors: the unseen threats in the darkness, never knowing whether people were the enemy or on his side, a land thick with vegetation and menace. He began to drink, then to take drugs, but nothing blocked the fear that kept his body and mind wound tight. Nothing blocked the grief from watching his brothers in arms die, or the guilt he felt that he was left alive.

After he'd served his country, he was abandoned again to face his nightmares and substance abuse problems on his own. With no family to turn to, he ended up living on the streets.

I did what I could for Mikey. I helped him apply for government benefits. Getting off the streets is hard work, and the hurdles to assistance are next to impossible to jump. Mikey didn't know which forms he needed to fill out. He didn't have access to a printer or a typewriter. He didn't even have a place where he could sit down with pen and paper. I let him come to my office, and I gave him an evaluation. We filled out his paperwork together. Mikey ended up receiving government benefits to get him off the streets, and mental health treatment through the VA Health Benefits System.

Mikey would always be fighting substance abuse and the wounds of war. But at least now that he was getting the aid he needed, he had more of a chance.

Mikey later found his mother, but she wasn't interested in having a relationship with him. He forgave her, but she would never be a mother to him. He never discovered why she left him that day. Maybe she couldn't handle his behavior. Maybe she just had too many children.

The tape of that moment still played in his head sometimes. Years later, he still pictured the car driving away into the dust, his brothers and sisters waving from the rear window.

But at least that tape wasn't all-consuming any longer. At least Mikey had the prospect of a new life.

For many of the men and women enduring homelessness I talked to, however, life was still about standing alone on a road, watching the rest of the world move on without them. They were abandoned by their families, by our country, and they were never certain why. I made it my mission to help where I could.

Mikey told me that people on the streets carry their home with them in their hearts. They may be houseless but they are not homeless. They may be dirty (it's hard not to be on the streets), they may be addicted to some substance or another, they may be yelling in psychic anguish, but they carry the potential for something better. They still have their hearts, and where there's a single heart, Mikey believed, there is a home. He always remembered a pillow in his adoptive mother's home that read, "Home is where the heart is."

* * *

Making the decision to step in and help those dealing with homelessness was a lot easier because someone had done so much to help me. I'd worked hard to get my degree and earn my license, but I'd had the support of a loving man at my side.

While I was a student at UCLA, I had to hustle to

support myself. I was studying and working several jobs. One of my gigs was to demonstrate a Japanese vitamin drink at trade shows for a man named Kenichi Nakamura. He needed additional help setting up a new office, so I started working part-time for him. One day I jokingly asked him, "Do you think this company will ever make enough money to pay me more?" I couldn't bear to ask for a raise when the product was not selling.

In his generous fashion, Kenichi offered to introduce me to a Japanese businessman who owned the office plaza where we worked.

Kenichi explained, "He's doing business here, but his English isn't good. He wants to be able to talk to people without an interpreter."

I had never taught English. I didn't want another job, but I'd always loved Japan, especially after I became interested in the macrobiotic diet developed by George Oshawa, a Japanese philosopher. I was already working more than one job and going to school full-time, but I thought I could find a few hours a week to help him. And I could use the money. Maybe I could learn a little more about Japan in exchange.

"There's just one thing," Kenichi said before my first English lesson. "Don't date him. He's a playboy."

I met Hiroshi Tanaka, or Hiro, as I later called him, one afternoon in an empty classroom at UCLA. He walked in, impeccably dressed in a suit. He bowed to me. I took a deep breath and decided to start with a simple conversation. "Hello," I said, "I'm Lorin Lindner."

"Hello, Lorin Lindner," he said slowly and carefully.

We sat down and began our first lesson. We learned

using books but also through talking—"broken English," he called it.

He wasn't loud or showy, but somehow you could sense he was powerful. Every time Hiro came to class, he had a different woman with him. I'm not sure if they were secretaries, interpreters, or girlfriends. He really did seem like a playboy.

Hiro was busy. It turned out he didn't own just the office building, but also restaurants, an import-export company, golf courses, and real estate. Hiro would entertain friends at business openings by renting entire hotels, providing gifts for all the guests.

He never bragged about his accomplishments or missed an appointment because of his schedule. He was always polite and respectful.

As he learned English, I learned about him. He told me things about Japanese culture I didn't know. I learned about the romantic sounds of the koto, the spare beauty of Japanese poetry, and the culture's respect for nature. He had traveled throughout the world, and he told me about the rest of Asia, Europe, and South America. I realized that he hadn't just been lucky in his commercial endeavors; he had a great mind.

He was also a very handsome man.

Six months after starting classes, he handed me a note, probably written by one of his assistants: "Do you want to go to a Dodgers' game with me?"

Of course I did.

He loved baseball. The enthusiasm on his face was infectious. Even though I'd never been much of a fan of organized sports, I found myself rooting along with him.

Hiro became the only man in my life. I told him about Kenichi's warning about him being a playboy. "You have to watch out for me," Hiro would joke. "I'm your playboy." We were together for nearly ten years.

While I was still a student at UCLA, Hiro helped me buy the condo in Westwood so I could walk or bike to school. He also insisted I trade in my old hippie van and bought me a more sensible vehicle. I drove that car and lived in that condo for the next twenty years.

We traveled quite a bit. He took me to Japan, and to other countries in Asia. Once, I told him that I wished he'd take me dancing, so we flew to Argentina and danced the tango. Another time we went to Carnival in Rio de Janeiro—for the weekend.

Hiro's one request of me was that I become a doctor. He didn't care if it was a doctorate in psychology or a medical degree. He simply encouraged me to pursue this goal because he knew it mattered to me.

He respected my opinions. He knew of my love for horses—anyone who knows me does—and suggested I go to the local riding stable. I wanted to badly, but I couldn't do it. I had become too aware of what horses at "hack" barns go through, hour after hour with strangers on their backs; I couldn't do that to them. Once he understood my objections, he never asked me to ride again. He also accommodated my vegan diet everywhere we traveled. Because I didn't want to burden the planet with one more person, he even got a vasectomy. He treated me as if my wishes mattered more than anything else in the world.

Hiro felt it was his role to help the woman in his life. As an independent woman, I was reluctant to accept financial help, but Hiro convinced me that I was helping him as much as he was helping me. He was worried about where I lived and about my driving a van held together with duct tape and luck. I liked having someone to look out for me. Our relationship was what I wanted at that time in my life, though I knew it wouldn't last. When we drove up the Pacific Coast Highway, he would point across the ocean and say wistfully: "Just over there . . . Japan." Hiro stayed in Los Angeles until I finished graduate school, and then he chose to go back to his country. His obligation to me, something of profound importance to a Japanese man of his generation, was completed. This concept of *giri* is foundational in Japanese culture, and Hiro would often bemoan the fact that "American-style" love did not encompass his sense of dedication and self-sacrifice. Whatever the reasons for his help and commitment, I was deeply grateful to him and always will be.

I missed him when he was gone. Maybe he's part of the reason Sammy's isolation touched me so much. I knew what it was like to feel alone.

Hiro gave me financial independence. Few of my friends were so lucky. When I started my practice, I had no debt and I owned my own home. I had the freedom to live my life as I wanted, and that is precisely what I set out to do. I didn't have to struggle to build my career by working long days at a large practice, but I felt a responsibility to give because so much had been given to me.

The decision to give back paid off. One day, I got a phone call. It was Otis, one of the formerly homeless men I'd worked with. Otis had been diagnosed with bipolar disorder with psychotic features. He once spent three days straight on the

swings at the playground, unable to sleep. After a manic epi-
sode passed, he would sleep in short spurts during the day,
when it was relatively safe, and then he'd wander the streets
at night.

"Dr. Lindner," he said, "guess where I'm calling from?"

I could hear his smile over the line. I couldn't help smiling myself. "Somewhere good?" I asked. It sounded like the
lottery, a new girlfriend, and a puppy rolled into one.

"My apartment," he paused, letting it sink in. "All mine."

We were silent for a moment.

"This is my first phone. My first call. I just wanted to say
thank you."

He had been disabled for over twenty years, and he'd
never had any hope of getting any sort of help. I was so
relieved the Social Services Administration saw his need
as well.

"I'm taking my medication. I'm doing okay. Now I want
to pay you back," he said.

"That's your money. My payment is knowing you're
doing well."

This feeling was better than money. My throat tightened.
I had studied psychotherapy to make a difference in people's
lives, but I hadn't expected to make such profound changes
so quickly.

I hung up the phone and sat down and cried.

When I walked around Westwood, homeless men would
wave and shout, "That's my doctor. Hey, Doc!" Word had
gotten around, especially from Mikey. He seemed to talk to
everyone. One afternoon, I locked up the office and headed
home. I was looking forward to going to a new restorative
yoga class many of my friends were raving about. I knew

Mango and Sammy would soon scurry to meet me, and I'd feel the calming touch of their feathers. I was done with talking for the night.

A man was standing in the shelter of a closed-up shop entrance. "You're the doctor who talks to the homeless, right?" he asked. I thought, Mikey, you know better than to send people my way at this hour.

"I'll be happy to see you tomorrow," I said to this stranger. "It's late. Let's talk then."

"I just need a couple of minutes."

"Tonight is really not the best for me."

"Please, Doc."

So I listened. Who knew how desperate he was and what would happen if I turned him away? He told his story, and it was a familiar one. He was a Vietnam veteran and just hadn't been able to adjust to life back in the United States. He'd started drinking, then taking drugs, and now he didn't know where to turn. He'd never been homeless before and he was afraid. Could I help him?

Something hit me. I don't know why I didn't see it sooner. Many of the men and women I talked to were veterans. Most had served in the Vietnam War. They were suffering from post-traumatic stress disorder (PTSD) caused by combat, but, without proper help, they were self-medicating. The diagnosis of PTSD didn't enter the *Diagnostic and Statistical Manual of Mental Disorders (DSM-III)* until 1980. Even though men and women have suffered from these symptoms as long as there have been warring humans (people might have called it "shell shock" or "battle fatigue," but it was the same problem), the diagnosis was controversial. Veterans were going undiagnosed and untreated, bearing the burden of their wounds alone.

Drugs and alcohol dampened the symptoms, but they never went away. Soon they were addicts. They lost their jobs, their homes, and their families. They ended up on the streets, with not just their original problems holding them back, but also the daily indignities of homelessness keeping them from recovering.

Imagine losing your home because of the problems that come with substance abuse. You can't keep a job, and you spend any savings you have. You can't pay your rent. At first, you crash on the couches of friends and family. But people with drug and alcohol dependency aren't easy to live with. Maybe there are too many late nights, too many lost tempers, maybe even stealing, and soon you've worn out your welcome, and you're on the streets.

You no longer have an address to give to potential employers or even to your friends and family. You don't have a bed. You don't have a toilet. You have just a few things: something to use as a bedroll, something to protect you from the rain and cold, a toothbrush and a cup. But you have nowhere to keep even these small belongings. The police and city workers will throw your things away if you leave them for a few minutes. Or someone will steal them. Just taking basic care of your body is a struggle. Sometimes restaurants and other businesses will let you use their bathrooms, but often you have nowhere to go. City police don't want you living outside, so they start arresting you for loitering, public urination, trespassing: the crimes of not having a place to live. Soon you have a criminal record, and your chances of crawling out of the hole you're in are even worse.

These homeless men had served our country. I had been against the Vietnam War, and I'd protested along with others in the sixties, but I was not against the men and women who'd fought. I had a friend who'd been drafted out of high school. If I'd been a man, maybe I'd have been in his shoes. I'd heard about the horrors the soldiers faced. These traumas were actual wounds and often caused PTSD.

I believed I owed it to my fellow men and women to give something back. My friends thought I was wasting my career by keeping my practice small while seeing homeless people on the side. They were wrong. That practice led me to my calling. I cared for all my clients, but I could see immediate, lasting changes with the homeless that weren't as clear in other clients. I could help these people in tangible ways. I saw that with Otis and Mikey. I knew, though, that working with the homeless one by one wasn't enough. The need was enormous. The problem was not one that a single person could handle.

I went home from that fateful meeting with that young, homeless man on the sidewalk and wrote a letter to every one of my legislators and all the media outlets I could think of. What was being done about homeless veterans and what could I do to help?

The governor's office was the first to respond, and his staff put me in touch with someone who shared my dream. His name was John Keaveney, and he had devoted his life to helping homeless veterans.

FIVE

New Directions

The moral power of an army is so great that
it can motivate men to get up out of a trench
and step into enemy machine-gun fire.

—JONATHAN SHAY, *Achilles in Vietnam: Combat Trauma*
and the Undoing of Character

Several days before I met John Keaveney, in 1990, I dreamed
I took over an enormous vacant building and invited in formerly "houseless" families. Those who knew carpentry,
plumbing, and electrical repair used their skills and taught
others. People watched each other's children. They planted
gardens to provide food. Everyone came together for an
evening meal in a huge communal kitchen. I knew I was
dreaming, but it felt real.

At our first meeting, I described the dream to John. He
looked askance, as if he thought I was mocking him.

"How do you know my wife?" he asked.

"What do you mean? I don't know your wife," I replied.
What was he talking about?

"No one else except her knows about the dream I just

had," he said, and he went on to describe a dream very like mine. This partnership, I thought, was meant to be.

A loud and temperamental native of Scotland, John Keaveney had sailed away with the merchant marines when he was sixteen. He had been in fights on the streets of Glasgow and needed to escape. After slipping off a ship and joining his aunt in the United States, he kept fighting, and his aunt kicked him out. He joined the army, was granted American citizenship, and served two tours of duty in Vietnam. During the Vietnam War, soldiers could easily get alcohol, and it was often shipped in with a unit's supplies. Some units issued it to soldiers along with other standard rations. John drank his share but soon wanted something stronger, and he turned to heroin. As long as the troops followed orders, many officers turned a blind eye to drug use among the enlisted men. Some estimates of heroin addiction among American soldiers in Vietnam are as high as 20 percent. By the time he left Vietnam, John was an addict.

He had been a tough young man when he entered the military, and now, settling in Los Angeles, he was angry and addicted. When vets like John came home, many people acted as if they were the enemy. Even the VA healthcare system did not provide appropriately for their needs at first. Veterans waited days for a ten-minute appointment with a physician. Hospitals were overcrowded. Employers weren't hiring veterans, and the government wasn't helping the men and women who'd served to start over. Men like John were in and out of jail, still fighting battles even though they were back home.

John turned his anger into action. He staged a hunger strike. He organized protests. He held his VA social worker hostage at knifepoint to demand more services for Vietnam veterans. A SWAT team stormed in to rescue the man from John's clutches. The social worker, a veteran himself, chose not to press charges. I suspect he knew that John would never really hurt him, though at the time he must have been petrified.

That social worker recommended a rehab program at the VA, and it, along with the hard work John was willing to do to stay clean and sober, saved his life. John began putting the energy and toughness he'd once used for fighting into helping other veterans. In 1988, when the program he had gone through at the VA shut down because of budget cuts, John acted. He knew there were thousands of homeless and addicted veterans. He couldn't let other vets suffer when he'd been saved. He had been there and had needed that help himself. Like me, John had had someone to help him, and, like me, he felt compelled to hold out his hand and help others.

John began knocking on nearly every door at the West Los Angeles VA Healthcare Center. This VA is a massive property, almost four hundred acres. It is home to a large hospital, a theater, a baseball stadium, and even a golf course. There had to be room, John thought, for homeless and addicted veterans as well. He knew there was a 150,000-square-foot building that hadn't been used in seventy-five years. Homeless veterans had broken in through windows and crumbling doors and were already squatting there. There was no running water and no electricity. Rotten floors and stairwells could collapse at any time.

"There are no homeless veterans," West Los Angeles VA officials told John.

I knew there were dozens of veterans living under the freeway just outside the VA's gates. They slept there while waiting for their follow-up appointments, often booked several weeks or even months out. I met one man who walked fifteen miles to his appointments because he didn't have a car. There was no sense walking back to Pasadena when he'd have to be back at the VA a few days later, so he slept outside.

Of course there were homeless veterans. The evidence was all around us.

VA officials weren't convinced by the homeless living under the overpasses near the campus and even in the buildings on the grounds. They needed proof they were veterans. John teamed up with Toni Reinis, a demure, quiet woman who nonetheless is a strong advocate for those suffering from homelessness. She had begun by running a food pantry and shelter, then went on to urge the Los Angeles Homeless Services Authority to conduct research on the population of homeless people in Los Angeles. LAHSA found that on any given night there were over 84,000 homeless people in Los Angeles County, and, of these, approximately 33 percent were veterans. That was 27,800 homeless veterans, more than in any other city in the country. With those staggering numbers, Toni had the ammunition to help us convince the West Los Angeles VA to tackle the problem of homelessness.

John, Toni, and I went to meetings at the VA, and many professionals in the social work and mental health departments wanted to help. Others did not. Part of their reluctance was that the VA campus sits in the middle of one of the wealthiest areas in Los Angeles. Bringing homeless people in would not sit well with its outspoken neighbors. As Toni and I knew, though, the homeless were already there. Toni lived in nearby Brentwood, and she used her influence to get the neighborhood associations to agree to have a homeless veterans program in their neighborhood.

John contacted his fellow veterans and the organizations representing them. He called the media. They already knew him from his earlier protests.

The 150,000-square-foot building John had found was old and decrepit, useless, and even dangerous. The VA had let it sit empty for seventy-five years, but wouldn't let us have it. "You will need to get an act of Congress," the VA told us.

Do not challenge John Keaveney. He went to Washington, DC, and he got that act of Congress. John got a fifty-year lease on the building for one dollar and founded New Directions, naming it in honor of the program that had helped him recover.

But the VA still put up roadblocks. Next, it said the building didn't meet modern earthquake standards, and it required that we retrofit it to meet current regulations. The cost? Eleven million dollars.

Toni knew architects and engineers and managed to raise the money and reduce the costs to three million. Such a bargain. Finally, we were ready to start construction.

While John and Toni were working their miracles, another miracle happened. An associate of John's, also a veteran, donated a four-bedroom house not far from the VA. The larger building on the VA campus wouldn't be open until construction was completed, but we could begin to help a few veterans right then. John immediately enlisted my aid. In addition to housing we would be providing drug and alcohol counseling, trauma recovery, group therapy, and a fellowship program based on AA. I wrote the entire program manual and all the protocols in a week because John was in a hurry to get started. I served as the program's psychologist, pro bono, of course, since there were no funds to pay anyone at this point. Hiro's generosity made it possible for me to offer help without having to ask for money.

We could help twelve veterans at a time, sleeping three to a room. Veterans would stay up to a year, long enough to make substantive changes in their lives. We were making a difference, but we had to turn away most veterans who needed help. Our waiting list was long, so we did everything within our collective power to get that big building open at the VA.

Finally, in 1997, we officially opened New Directions, a 156-bed, one-year residential treatment facility. Since we now had this large building for men, we converted the original four-bedroom house into a facility for women. John asked me to be the clinical director. My friends had said I was throwing my career away by "working for the homeless." Now I held a post with great responsibility, simply doing what I loved.

The West Los Angeles VA had claimed there were "no homeless veterans," but we were full from day one. To give the VA credit, though, it did not take long for it to see this was a long-neglected need. Within two years, the VA offered us a second building for the treatment of veterans who have dual diagnoses—mental illness as well as substance dependence. Within four years, the VA was being recognized for its work and winning awards of excellence for its treatment of homeless veterans.

From the start all of the staff were spending most of our

waking hours at New Directions. We needed additional staff desperately; one of the first people John hired was the social worker he'd once held hostage. John was the kind of person who could hold a knife to someone's throat one day and have that person working for him the next.

I spent at least twelve hours a day doing screenings and intakes, biopsychosocial evaluations, individual and group therapy, and family reunification groups until I could hire and train additional staff. Because of my workload, Sammy and Mango were apart from me for longer periods of time than I had ever left them previously. I knew I shouldn't leave them alone for so long. The veterans were my responsibility, but I'd taken Sammy and Mango for life. I began toting them to work. I thought I was bringing them to alleviate their boredom from being alone in my little condo, but of course it also felt good being with my feathered family, and it eased the tension. I was spending all my time wearing my professional mask. With Sammy and Mango, I could relax. I could be myself, not the doc. I could take a breath and have a few moments of peace and calm.

Little did I know the impact these birds would have on the residents of The House, as we affectionately called the massive building that held our program. I already knew they could bring joy into a person's life, but I was about to find out that they could do so much more.

* * *

I placed two spacious cages outside my door and a T-stand in my office. The cage doors were usually open, allowing the birds freedom to roam.

Nearly every veteran in The House stopped by to say

hello to Sammy and Mango. The men shared oranges and apples with the birds. They scratched their backs. They told them they were beautiful. Talk about spoiled! In return, I noticed some of the veterans getting positive feedback from those two. From soft avian cooing to loud human expressions, Sammy and Mango always had something to say.

"C'mere, give me a beer" was still one of Sammy's favorite phrases. In a building full of recovering addicts, that's not necessarily the best thing to say. The men would laugh, though, so I decided she wasn't hurting anyone's recovery.

With an outstretched foot, Mango tried to climb onto everyone's passing shoulder. "I wuv you," he would exclaim. Those stoic soldiers would suddenly be smiling like children, totally unguarded.

If he couldn't hitch a ride by shoulder, Mango would scramble down from his cage and skitter across the perpetually freshly polished floor—the men were ex-military, after all. He'd climb up any passing pant leg and repeat with emphasis: "Hewwoooo, I wuvvv you."

Recovery was serious work, but Mango helped bring some lightness to the day. Most of the men were glad to give him a little ride.

Mango's cage was near the desk where the men doing their construction training would sign in and out. Mango loved it. He'd climb into their tool belts, examining the contents with his beak and long, nimble toes. He was always a boys' boy.

A few days after Mango arrived, the men around the construction desk started complaining about things going missing.

"Hey, man, I've got to sign in my hours. Quit taking the pen."

"You're losin' it, bro," someone answered. "I didn't take your pen."

That's the sound of PTSD: accusations and mistrust. Mango let the voices roll off his feathers. He didn't make a peep.

"Who took my screwdriver? Ask if you want my things."

"Dude, I know you've been in my tool belt. Stay away."

The arguments went on for days. The men were starting to think one of them was a compulsive thief and liar. Everyone was a suspect.

Mango would preen himself and ignore the fracas a little too intently. He looked like someone avoiding making eye contact with a teacher. Maybe, I thought, we'd better check the prankster out.

When we searched his cage, a large structure with plenty of room for a parrot to stretch out, we found out where all the missing things had gone. Mango had stashed pens, pencils, and small tools under his newspapers. Parrots are smart enough to be curious, but they're also smart enough to be mischievous.

We gave the items back. The men apologized to each other.

Mango hadn't meant to teach a lesson, but he had. Veterans with PTSD can be quite suspicious. They often believe others aren't trustworthy. When their things started to disappear, they were quick to blame the other men, quick to think there was a thief sifting through their things. It was not officially therapy, but I think it helped the men. A bird couldn't possibly be out to get them. He just liked his toys. The guys were able to laugh at their suspicions.

I was glad Sammy and Mango were getting attention while I spent all these hours doing my work. They thrived, showing off for the men. They hardly ever called out anymore. It was a huge relief to see them happy, but having my feathered family in my office was still only a convenience.

That was about to change. The two strands of my life, animals and therapy, weren't separate at all.

One day I led yet another fruitless group therapy session. The marines, Navy SEALs, and Army Rangers sat silent and taciturn. How could I be failing them so badly? They had seen death and destruction. Surely psychotherapy for forty-five minutes each week couldn't scare them. I was offering them an opportunity to get their feelings out, to work through their pain; this is how I'd been trained to help. I had to ask myself if I was helping at all.

I had long doubted this one-size-fits-all approach to therapy. Traditional therapies can be effective if conducted by a competent, well-trained practitioner. There's an overabundance of "therapists," but unfortunately not all of them have the proper education, training, and supervision. Even if a therapist does have these things, traditional therapies may not be appropriate for all people. I could see for myself that these men weren't helping each other heal; they thought group therapy was a waste of time.

Even in private sessions, many were closed off, difficult to reach. They didn't want to discuss their lives with some woman not steeped in military tradition. Talking about emotional problems, and finding solutions to those problems, is frowned on in the military. Soldiers ignore pain, push it down, and keep their eyes on the task at hand.

"Keep on moving, keep your mouth shut, and don't look back" was a time-honored motto. After years of training to be stoic, they weren't going to open up to me just because I was a psychologist.

More than that, our modern military is diverse, and different groups of people seek mental health remedies in different ways. While most conventional psychotherapies derive from treating affluent, educated, white patients, people from other backgrounds might be resistant to the traditional psychotherapy model. Many of the men in New Directions were working-class and African American or Hispanic. Talking to a preacher, *curandero*, or esteemed community leader might be fine, but talking to a therapist was unmanly. I was an educated white woman, foreign to their experience, and suspect. I knew that, to many of them, my face blended with those of correction officers, prison therapists, and teachers; I looked the same as the people who'd labeled them and talked down to them their entire lives.

I did well with some veterans, but others would cross their arms and look away from me. If they answered my questions, they'd do so in the fewest words possible. I wanted to help them find ways to solve their problems on their own, without drugs. I had no intention of talking down to them or lecturing. I should have been a guide on the path they had to walk, but we weren't able to get far enough along in therapy for them to realize that. We weren't able to redirect their behaviors and thoughts into more positive directions; in fact, we weren't communicating at all.

That changed the day Willy came into my office. I'd seen

him once before, and he'd spent the session with his arms crossed, staring out the window. He had been a trained sharpshooter, and the military had selected him as a sniper; he would not discuss his experience in combat with anyone. Willy's mother was a prostitute, and though I sensed he respected her a great deal, he still felt a lot of shame. Building a rapport with a woman was going to be difficult. Not that he was going to talk about it.

We'd been able to get Willy out of prison as part of a program to help formerly homeless veterans. His hearing was held in the New Directions building, where an official Drug Court, complete with a judge and bailiffs, was stationed, and he went straight from there to the program. Allowing veterans to enter our program kept them out of prison, saving the government money and freeing up prison space, and it gave them a second chance. These men and women had multiple infractions on their records, many of them stemming directly from their homelessness (possession of a shopping cart, sleeping in a car, open container violations). They ended up with long prison times because of mandatory sentencing laws. Willy was convicted of possession of a small amount of crack cocaine, a crime that gave him a much longer sentence than an equivalent amount of powder cocaine would have. He'd racked up several years behind bars. We agreed to take him into the program, and he agreed to get clean.

He wanted to get out of prison. He wanted to stay off drugs. He just didn't think I could help him. He had to attend therapy as part of the program, but he wasn't about to put in any effort. I was nothing more than another hurdle he had to leap over.

I'm not sure why, but I felt as if it would be a good idea to have Mango join in our second session. I never could have predicted what happened next.

I placed Mango on his T-stand in the corner of my office. Willy smiled, an actual, natural smile.

"Who's that?" he asked.

"Mango," I said. "He's a cockatoo. Would you like to meet him?"

"I'm not touching no bird," he said, but I noticed he was still smiling at Mango.

Mango did a little dance, bobbing up and down. He was a bit of a diva and loved getting attention.

"Does he talk?" Willy asked.

"Let's see," I said, an idea forming in my head. "Mango," I said, "I love you."

"I wuv you," Mango said wistfully. Willy laughed.

Mango walked up to Willy. Willy laughed again. He leaned back in his chair, arms relaxed. I saw that there was something about Mango that bypassed his defenses. Willy was open, suddenly unscreened.

He'd claimed he wouldn't touch a bird, but he let Mango crawl right up his leg and into his lap.

"How'd you get him?" he asked as he groomed Mango's feathers. Willy was a natural.

Psychologists aren't supposed to disclose details of their lives to patients, and there are good reasons for that. I wasn't going to give Willy too much information about my life, but I wanted to build a therapeutic relationship.

"I took him in. He's a rescue."

Willy nodded.

"How long will he live?" he asked. When people meet the

birds, they almost always ask their names, whether they talk, and how long they live.

"Fifty to seventy years. It depends."

He whistled. "That's a long time in a cage."

Mango hadn't been in a cage. I wondered why Willy would say that. I made a note in my head.

"I don't leave him in a cage except to sleep. I wouldn't keep an animal locked up."

Willy nodded. He smiled.

And we talked. It felt as if I'd passed some kind of test. Willy trusted me, at least a little bit, and that was a good start.

"Will I see him again?" Willy said as our appointment ended.

Oh yes, Willy would be seeing Mango again.

* * *

The healing power of animals had been obvious to me even before Willy spoke to Mango. We evolved in a natural world full of animals. Why wouldn't they be an important part of our well-being? They are integral to the landscape of childhood and they connect us to something basic in our natures. They give us joy.

When I was a child, grieving for a mother who was absent with frequent illnesses, going to my sister's home in the country gave me solace. I rode horses for hours. I spoke to them as I groomed them. I felt I understood them.

Before Sammy and Mango came into my life, I hadn't realized I had grown a little lonely. I loved having them there when I awoke, even though they never let me sleep in. I loved having two creatures to care for. They filled a need I hadn't even been aware I had.

I knew that when we bond with animals, we connect to the world at an emotional level. What I didn't understand was how effective they would be at helping me build a rapport with my clients. They helped create the sense of safety and trust upon which a therapeutic relationship is built. Sammy and Mango improved the veterans' communication skills by getting them to talk, and the birds also helped the veterans increase their ability to empathize and forgive.

I began bringing Sammy and Mango into my office regularly. As we are, parrots are social creatures and, as for us, conflict is part of their relationships. A big part of my work with the veterans was teaching them to resolve these conflicts in productive ways. These are men who often grew up with anger and aggression in their lives. As adults, they went through the horrors of combat, fought for survival on the streets, and sometimes suffered the institutional brutality so common in prison. Like all men and women, they needed to assert their identity and protect themselves. Unfortunately, they hadn't learned or weren't willing to try nonviolent ways of doing so. Learning to solve conflicts in a nonconfrontational way was a large part of their therapy. I could use the parrots to help with that learning.

Sammy was a mommy's girl, and she wanted Mango to know it. The two didn't outright fight, but Sammy would needle Mango. She wanted to show him who came first. She'd try to edge Mango off the perch, slowly getting into his space until he had no room.

"How do you think Mango feels?" I asked Willy one day.

"I think they're going to fight," he said.

"What do you think Mango needs?"

Willy looked puzzled. He clearly thought I was some kind

of fool for asking. "He needs his space. He needs to fight her back."

We both watched the birds quietly. Mango leaned a bit on Sammy, let her know that she was pushing him too far, and Sammy hopped back a few inches. There was no biting, not even a squawk. "It seems they've worked it out," I said.

Mango had held his ground, he'd asserted his needs, but he'd kept his beak to himself. I knew Willy could appreciate that.

"Yeah," he said, "I guess."

It was a start. For Willy, relationships had been about conflict and aggression. The birds had their conflicts, but they worked them out without fighting. I was able to use them as models of positive behaviors, and because we were just discussing some birds, it didn't sound like lecturing. The men didn't need another authority figure giving advice, but they could observe a real-life model of behaving differently. Social Learning Theory describes this perfectly: learning occurs in a social context strictly through observation or imitation. But the models are typically human; perhaps animals were even better teachers. Animals aren't threatening. Animals aren't judgmental. Animals just are.

Willy could watch the parrots, and he could trust them. He would talk with me about the birds and their behavior. It was easier for him to speak about an animal than it was for him to speak about his own life.

"How do you think Mango is feeling today?" I'd say.

"He doesn't seem good."

Mango was acting normally, prying open seeds, grooming Sammy, studying the people in the room.

"Why do you think that?" I asked.

"He's angry."

"How do you know that?"

Willy talked about Mango, about how Mango felt disrespected, about how some people invaded his space. We talked about what strategies Mango could use to deal with those problems without hurting himself and others. I don't know if Willy realized he was talking about himself and that he was projecting his feelings onto Mango. It didn't matter as long as he was learning.

Before long, Willy was making real progress. He never discussed his work as a sniper—he made it clear that he would never talk about that part of his life with others—but he did talk about moving forward. Other veterans made progress as well when I brought the parrots into their sessions. The veterans had the birds at their back, and with their calming and fun presence, they were starting to heal. Maybe I was onto something.

Over time, the veterans grew to trust me. Laughter and conversations no longer stopped when I sat down with the men outside of sessions. They'd even help me catch up on what they were discussing. I wasn't just another white, female face. I was a friend. Twice a week, all the members of The House had to take part in group discussions about their recovery. The groups were peer-run, but I'd sometimes enter to deliver a message. When I walked into the meeting, all the men would stand up. I knew I'd earned their respect.

When John Keaveney, a fellow veteran and drug addict, walked into the room, he would demand: "Sit the hell down and shut the hell up." Every one of them listened, and they loved him. They knew he would do anything for them, including lay down his life.

I'm too cute for my own good!

All photos are from Serenity Park unless otherwise noted.

Army veteran Jesse with his wingman, blue and gold macaw Bacardi.

Liz Black

Sid gives one of his lofty looks for the camera.

Matt and Lorin. The love found at Serenity Park is bound by a poem read by actor James Cromwell.

A home is not a home unless it is made by your own design. Ruby carves out her own front door.

Cashew, the biggest heart in the smallest body.

Bobbi Socks.

Buzz Varley

It was love at first flight for Sammy and Matt.

Dinner is served. Veterans at Serenity Park are serious about the forage trays.

Dandy is our biggest flirt.

Joey never lets Ruby out of his sight.

(*opposite*) The unspoken word felt in the embrace of a wounded hero.

George. It takes all kinds at Serenity Park.

The guys would get up in each other's faces and yell. There was a lot of chest-thumping. They'd cuss each other out and create new and inventive ways to insult each other's manhood. But it was all done with a pat on the back. They were brothers. It was in times like those that I was glad I grew up in what was then a tough area of New York City—Corona, Queens—and wasn't afraid of a little rowdiness. They respected the fact that I didn't back down and could talk just as loudly and roughly as they did.

The entire group shared communal meals in the large dining hall. I would join the men and ask them to speak informally. The amount of caring and compassion was overwhelming, and I saw the benefits of working the Twelve Step Program in each of their lives. If someone was struggling, thinking about drugs constantly, the guys would talk it out and try to help.

"I keep thinking I could use just one beer. Just one," a man would say.

"It always starts with one, man," another would say. "Stay strong."

"Work your program. You've got this."

I just sat and listened. They didn't need my help.

If two people were arguing—inevitable in any group— they'd hash things out at the table. If a man was worried about health problems or a loved one back home, they'd try to figure out a solution. The guys were staying clean. They were talking to each other, using words and not fists. They showed one another respect.

If I did talk, they'd quiet down and listen. They'd nod. They seemed to care what I had to say.

Some of my colleagues still doubted the wisdom of

working with formerly homeless addicts. I pointed out that I had gone from pro bono shrink to clinical director of the program, but some friends still worried. The men in the program weren't businessmen struggling with minor depression or married couples disagreeing about finances; many had committed serious crimes. The military had trained them to kill. Their manners were rough, and they were often physically intimidating. I convinced some of my fellow professionals to attend the fun-filled talent shows and other events the vets put on each year, so they could see the progress the men were making, but they were still suspicious.

"Well, aren't you frightened? You work late into the night over there, and most of those guys are felons, after all," they'd say.

"Yes," I agreed. "I am afraid, afraid that if anyone from outside that building tried to mess with me, my veterans would kill him." My friends rolled their eyes.

The truth was that New Directions was a sanctuary for me as well as for the veterans. I went on to study to become certified in military psychology, posttraumatic stress disorder, and traumatic brain injury so I could help these men. I felt the parrots were helping as well. Bringing in Sammy and Mango had gone from a convenience for me to an important tool in my healing arsenal. Maybe, I thought, I could find a way for the birds to do more.

SIX

Finding Sanctuary

The secret of being miserable is to have leisure
to bother about whether you are happy or not.
The cure for it is occupation.

—GEORGE BERNARD SHAW, *Misalliance*

Bringing Sammy and Mango into the office was working out
for everyone, but sometimes I was forced to leave them at
home. One Friday, I had to attend meetings outside of the
VA Medical Center all day, so the birds had remained at the
condo. I didn't hesitate to bring them to the comforting environment of New Directions, but of course I'd never take
them along to a professional meeting.

Moments after I got home, there was a knock at the door.
Mango ran across the carpet to greet our visitor. He loved
company, any company.

It was my neighbor. Mango looked at him with one eye.
"Hewwo," he said. "I wuv you."

The neighbor sighed. "I was coming to complain about

the noise," he said, "but after that greeting, I guess I'll just go home."

Mango might not make for the quietest neighbor, but he was charming. The neighbor explained that while I was gone the birds screamed all day long.

I apologized, but it hurt to hear. Those weren't screams of joy; Sammy and Mango were lonely and crying out for their flock.

I loved Mango and Sammy, but they didn't belong in a condominium in Los Angeles. They needed a more natural environment, and my neighbors needed some peace and quiet. My home would feel empty, but I needed to make the proper decision. I hoped I hadn't held on to them too long because of my own need to be with them.

Parrots may be fascinating birds, but neighbors often don't think they make good pets. A friend of mine, Jeannie White, also had Moluccan cockatoos; we had been introduced because of our shared love of birds. She was having the same experience with her neighbors, but they had called the Department of Animal Services. She had received citations. She knew her birds couldn't live in a residential neighborhood, and she was searching for a sanctuary. There was one in Tucson, Arizona, but Jeannie loved her birds and wanted them closer.

We both realized many other parrot lovers must be experiencing the same thing. All birds deserve a place where they can feel the sunlight and call out as loudly as they want; it's in their nature. Some people can give parrots what they need, but if I was going to be gone twelve hours a day, I wasn't one of them. So Jeannie and I decided to found Earth Angel Parrot Sanctuary.

We discussed trying to create this new parrot sanctuary at the VA. The veterans would care for the birds, and, from what I'd seen with Willy and the other vets, I knew the birds could help the veterans. They might create a new kind of treatment together. Someday, I thought, I'd make it happen. But I had to be realistic. The birds needed a sanctuary right away, not years in the future.

"It took seven years to get New Directions started," I told Jeannie.

Jeannie knew her neighbors wouldn't be patient that long and that many other birds were in the same situation.

"Let's try somewhere else," she said.

I've always believed that you have to envision what you want and make it happen. We set out to build an oasis for our birds, even though we didn't have land or money, and that's what we did.

Jeannie found a 325-acre property in Ojai, California, about eighty-five miles from Westwood. John and Melody Taft, the owners, had made the land bloom with plants that thrived in an arid climate. Their garden was a paradise of green, and because their plantings were suited to the climate, it didn't overconsume water. The Tafts already had some aviaries, and they were willing to consider building more and bringing additional parrots to their enchanting and spacious property. The Tafts wanted more than just a garden; they wanted to create a place to educate others. People could learn about the plants and the animals. They'd see how to grow an environmentally responsible native garden in our unique climate. With Sammy, Mango, and the other birds, we could teach people that, in spite of their intelligence and beauty, parrots make poor

pets for a casual owner. With that education, the sanctuary would help to make itself obsolete. And it would cost
very little.

When we first made the trip to Ojai, in 1997, to meet
with these incredibly generous people, I realized how much
I wanted to live away from the big city. Ever since my sister
had married and moved to the country, I'd had the same
dream. My sister had let me run barefoot with her children
through the unmown grass. Nature became my home. When
I was six or seven, I envisioned my adult life with one special
horse and ten dogs. In my bedroom back then, in addition
to the dozens of Breyer horse models on a shelf, I had post-
ers of the breeds of dogs and horses on my walls. I had already decided which dogs I would have and what type of
horse. Most of all, I wanted no visible neighbors, at least not
human ones.

But I was too busy working at New Directions to leave
Los Angeles for country living. The dream would have to
wait. The birds, though, could have what I couldn't. They
could have a flock, as parrots are meant to. Maybe Sammy
would even find a mate; Mango had become more like an
annoying brother to her. I'd miss them, but the thought of
what they could have brought me joy.

"This would be a perfect place for the birds," I whispered
to my friend.

Amazingly, with the help of the Tafts, it fell into place
quickly. And once the word got out, people who wanted to
surrender their parrots began to call. Some were moving,
some had just had a baby, some had allergies, and some simply did not have the time for a bird. I had known there were

many parrots in need of a home, but I hadn't expected this volume of calls. We began building aviaries.

* * *

These were animals who needed healing, just like the vets. Some, like Sammy, had suffered the trauma of being wild-caught. Those bred in captivity often came from dirty, dark, overcrowded birdie mills and were then weaned far too early. The majority had been moved multiple times. Parrots would come to the sanctuary missing most of their feathers. They had been locked in cages with no companionship, room to move, or activities, and they had mutilated themselves to deal with stress. Others would lash out at any human contact. They'd learned to distrust humans, who reacted with screaming and even violence to normal bird behaviors. Many were undernourished, like Sammy was when I found her.

When the first aviaries were ready, it was time to move Sammy and Mango. Unlocking the door and hearing their joyful welcome was the brightest part of my evening. I was used to Sammy snuggling with me on the couch. My shoulder felt light without one of the birds riding on it. I even looked forward to laughing at Mango's latest work of mischief. I chatted with them on the drive, trying to keep the panic from rising in my voice. I wanted them to be calm when they saw their new home. I knew bringing them to Ojai was the right decision, but my stomach clenched thinking of leaving them. Knowing I was doing the right thing didn't make it easier. As I carried their cages from the car, my hands trembled. I walked into the aviary and let them out. It was a space large enough for two birds to roam, and Sammy and

Mango climbed about. I laughed to see how excited they were to explore their new space, but there were tears in my eyes.

Just like parents who send their children away to college, I was sick with worry. They were going from a condo to a large aviary surrounded by flowers and plants. They could feel the sun and wind on their feathers. I kept telling myself that moving was the best thing for them, and I never missed a visit.

Every weekend, I brought the veterans from New Directions to help with the construction of more aviaries and to visit the birds. I didn't bring them to save on labor costs, though that was a side benefit. Getting out in nature, having productive work, and interacting with the parrots would help them.

There was a lot of work to do installing perches and bottomless nest boxes in the aviaries. The bottomless boxes offered privacy but no place to lay eggs, so they discouraged the birds from breeding; there were already so many parrots in need of homes, and we didn't want to add more. In the dry, dusty California summer, the men needed plenty of breaks. As they sat in the shade, they'd watch Sammy and Mango and the other birds. It didn't take long before even the newer men would approach the birds and talk.

Many of the birds were hand-reared and loved interacting with people. They raised their crests. They flapped their wings. When a bird is interested in you, she or he lets you know it. I explained to the men what the behaviors meant, and they smiled. For many, it had been a long time since anyone had genuinely welcomed them.

"Birds are not like dogs, who have been bred to give us affection," I told them. "They don't care to appease us or to stay in our good graces. If a bird capable of flight approaches you, it's because that bird is truly interested." I made sure the men understood the birds were responding positively because they liked having the men around. They were wanted, a great feeling for formerly homeless people used to being seen as a nuisance or just overlooked. I was pleasantly surprised by the reactions the birds got as well. These tough marines, sailors, and soldiers were practically cooing back to them with soft, calm, and tender voices:

"Hello back to you, pretty bird."

"Who's a good bird?"

"I love you, too."

I never made emotional inroads that fast in a clinical setting. The hard barrier around the men's hearts was cracking. Animals provide a healthy dose of antidepressants, a client of mine used to say. I could see this truth in action at Ojai.

At the end of each day, we sat on the grass in a circle. It was a time of rest for the vets and a time to peacefully discuss what had gone right and what had gone wrong during our work there. Sammy went up a nearby tree to watch the proceedings, but Mango wanted to get involved. I'd bring a little ball with a small rubber band wrapped around it for Mango to grab onto. Mango had his favorites at New Directions, and he avoided anyone who smelled of cigarettes. But when we sat in the circle, he'd make sure each man got his turn to play. He brought the ball up to the first man in the circle, retrieved the ball after it was thrown, and then walked over to the next man in the circle. He never skipped anyone. For men who'd often been overlooked, that little bit of attention meant something. It helped defuse any tensions that developed during the workday, but, more than that, it gave the men a taste of what it felt like to be valued—even if by a very self-important little cockatoo.

Once a month or so, I'd take Mango or Sammy home for an overnight visit. I think Sammy especially liked to have me all to herself. After a while, though, I noticed she was getting quite attached to another Moluccan cockatoo in Ojai. She did not come down from her perch as readily to see me, and I had to coax her to leave the aviary to come for a walk on my shoulder. It was hard to see my little girl moving on, but I had to let it happen; it was nature's course. I decided not to remove her as often so as not to disrupt that budding relationship.

So the next weekend it was Mango who came home. Going to and from Los Angeles to the sanctuary in Ojai, I'd drive with the veterans in the New Directions van. Mango loved to sit on the gearshift, slowly grooming himself. He'd balance on one leg and use the other to hold up his wing while he groomed the underside. Whenever the driver changed gears, Mango would grudgingly hold on with both legs, then he'd stand on one leg and begin grooming one wing again.

"Dr. Lindner," the driver that weekend pointed out, "that's just like you said."

"What's like I said, Rick?"

"Living in the moment. If we're always thinking about what's going to happen next, if we're worried about tomorrow, we're not living right now."

I knew that lesson. I often refer to Eckhart Tolle's *The Power of Now* in my treatment sessions, but I didn't understand what Rick meant.

"Well, this guy," he said, gesturing to Mango. "All he wants is to groom his feathers. He just perches up there and he goes at it. When we stop, he's got to hold on with both feet, but then he goes right back at it. Doesn't matter that we just stopped two minutes ago. Doesn't matter that we're going to have to stop two minutes from now. He just keeps grooming 'cause it feels good right now."

I never would have thought of it that way, but I saw what he meant. Mango was completely present. He didn't worry that an intersection was coming up and that he'd have to hold on. He didn't care that we'd just interrupted him. He needed to groom, so he groomed. He was right there, every second.

"He's focused on getting what he wants and he makes no bones about it," Rick said.

In my clinical work, many of the people I see have difficulty asking directly for their needs to be met in effective and appropriate ways. At some point in their lives they learned they probably wouldn't get what they needed anyway. Mango asks directly for what he wants all the time. There's no mistaking it. He lays his head right in your palm when he wants you to stroke him. He makes it look like asking for love is that easy, and that helps men like Rick see that it's worth a shot.

Not all the veterans were as persuaded that the birds valued affection—not by Mango, anyway. Some were suspicious of him, and for good reason. Like all wild animals, he had a mind of his own. He loved attention and petting, but if you stopped, he might latch onto your hand. Mango's beak could easily crush nuts; escaping his grip was a serious matter. Although this only happened twice, and nobody lost their digits, the vets started calling him "the Mangler." He didn't do any serious harm; he was sending the message that you needed to pay attention to him. Still, some kept their distance.

Mango didn't mind. Even though he'd run up to everyone and say he loved them, Mango cared about some people more than others. Parrots, like us, have their favorites.

Mango liked Tony, one of the new veterans, best of all. Like all the men at New Directions, he was a former substance abuser. Physically, he looked like a big, tough guy, not somebody you'd necessarily expect to be a cuddler. When he saw Tony coming, Mango would run to him, climb up onto his arm, and go limp. He'd lean his head into Tony's chest and hold out his wings just a bit. Tony would pet Mango in the space under his wings. From the look on Tony's face, it seemed Tony enjoyed petting Mango as much as Mango enjoyed being petted. The tough-guy scowl would disappear.

Mango got his grooming from Tony. Tony's large fingers carefully pinched and removed the protective casings on Mango's feathers, never coming near the sensitive blood vessels. With Mango, Tony had the perfect touch.

On one particular day, Mango was in my office and Tony was stroking his feathers.

Jack, another veteran, walked in. "Oh my God! That's Mango the Mangler," he shouted. "He goes for the jugular!"

Tony shrieked. Mango shrieked.

Men with PTSD tend to hate sudden noises. They have exaggerated startle reflexes. Tony jumped back and dropped the bird. Mango fluttered to the ground and darted under my chair.

"Whoa, Jack," I declared. "Don't scare him like that."

Mango and Tony had been having a nice moment together before someone told Tony he should be afraid. Tony quickly realized he'd been wrong. He'd petted Mango dozens of times and he'd never been bitten. I think he was more startled by and scared of Jack's yelling than he was of his friend Mango.

"I'm sorry, Mango," Tony said softly.

Mango, dragging his beak along the ground and clucking, slowly walked up to Tony. He thought he'd done something wrong, even if he had no idea what it was.

"It's okay, Mango," Tony said. Mango hesitated, but he crawled back up Tony's arm again and settled against his chest. All was forgiven.

"I think that bird has a crush on Tony," Jack said sheepishly.

Maybe Mango did have a crush; Tony and Mango most certainly had a bond. Mango wasn't the only one who benefitted from their time together. We all understand the comfort of a hug or petting a soft animal. Physical contact with another creature is tremendously healing. From lowered blood pressure, shorter surgical recovery times, and endorphin release, to just plain stress reduction, touch and caring help us physically as well as mentally.

Jack and Tony also learned something about judging those around them. Many of the guys at New Directions had been labeled: drug addict, criminal, mentally ill, homeless. They knew what it was to be defined. Mango had been labeled as well. I think it was eye-opening for Tony to catch himself jumping to conclusions when he heard another creature labeled. I know it was also good for both Tony and Mango that they could forgive each other so easily and so quickly.

For several years, I'd seen the veterans working with the birds, and I'd seen the positive impact on both. But they were miles away in Los Angeles, and I could bring them out to Ojai once a week at most. The problem was, there simply wasn't enough sustained contact.

If I were really to make a difference in their lives, I'd have to bring the birds to the VA. After helping get New Directions off the ground, I had been concerned about the time and effort it would take to build a parrot sanctuary at the VA. There would be permits and regulations. We'd have to hack our way through multiple levels of bureaucracy. We'd need money. That's why we'd gone to Ojai in the first place. It was a good temporary solution, but in the long term, if I was going to reach my goal of truly helping veterans, I'd need to change course. It was time to build a sanctuary at the VA.

* * *

After World War II, Karl Menninger, an early proponent of horticulture therapy, began to integrate gardening and time in nature into the treatment of returning veterans. He founded the Menninger Clinic, where he opened greenhouses and outdoor gardens. This approach spread to VA hospitals throughout the country. Local gardening groups volunteered to help teach veterans the skills they needed to garden themselves. To this day, a fifteen-acre therapeutic garden exists at the West Los Angeles VA. There, veterans with disabilities can find routine, responsibility, and respect in the form of work. Their compensation is minimal, since it is assumed they receive service-connected benefits for their disabilities from the VA. But the value of working with their hands and being creative is enormous.

In 2001, I chose this garden at the VA as the perfect site for a parrot and veteran sanctuary. I knew Ida Cousino, who had run the Vet's Garden for twenty-five years, from my work as clinical director at New Directions. Under her watch, veterans with drug and alcohol addictions tended the gardens and sold their produce to the public. They grew herbs, lettuces, flowers, and vegetables, all organically. The men did hard physical labor, but it got them back into a routine of work. After about a year, they would transition into jobs in the community.

Ida loved nurturing and caring for living things, and that included the veterans who came through her program. No birthday went uncelebrated under Ida's watch. No matter how busy she was with work and her own family, there was always a homemade cake to celebrate important occasions. If the men needed tools, work clothes, or boots, she made sure they got them. Ida cared for "her" garden and "her" veterans even when she later retired to Mazatlán, Mexico, to paint. She set up Friends of the Garden, a charitable organization, to make sure that her vision of healing work in nature continued when she was gone. She liked the fact that money would be coming from the community, not the government; she wanted people to take care of each other. Even after retirement, she was never really gone. If her veterans needed her, she was a quick plane ride away.

That day in 2001, I described to her how the veterans were reacting to the parrots, how a little bit of the walls around their hearts would crack by being around the birds. It was a way to take care of parrots who were homeless and traumatized and to heal veterans with the same problems:

truly birds of a feather. I told her I hoped to reach many more veterans by relocating the parrots to the VA campus.

Ida immediately saw the benefits this collaboration could provide for the veterans. Around this time, animal-assisted therapy was becoming a well-established field of study. Researchers demonstrated that animals helped people affected by crisis, ameliorated the behavioral symptoms of dementia (such as agitation and decreased sociality), and even stimulated the appetites of those living in nursing homes. Of course, animals have been providing care and comfort to humans for centuries, but now the therapeutic effects were substantiated by scientific studies. Ida was not surprised by the benefits animals provide and recognized that our relationship with them goes back to childhood, when animals are often our very first best friends.

There were already programs using healthy animals to help people in need of assistance. Guide dogs, for example, help the blind. There were also programs that paired humans and animals in need of different kinds of help, such as inmates socializing and training dogs for adoption. I wanted to do something different. I wanted Serenity Park to be a meeting place for both humans and birds who suffer from the same stress-induced disorders. Understanding and empathy could be so much greater when both participants had the same obstacles to overcome.

PTSD results from profound trauma: physical abuse, deprivation, torture, isolation, forced incarceration, or witnessing the loss, death, or threat of death of a loved one. All of these can occur in times of war, and they can occur during the capture, transport, and prolonged confinement of parrots in captivity.

Wild animals taken for captive use are forcefully separated from their families. Often, they witness their family's deaths in the process of capture. The young animals are transported in abominable conditions. When they do reach their destinations, they are often left alone in cages, isolated from any flock. They are often abused. Such trauma and deprivation in vulnerable and dependent animals leaves lasting psychological wounds.

An individual with PTSD reexperiences stressors, usually in the form of intrusive thoughts and flashbacks, avoids reminders of the trauma, and suffers hyperarousal. Because of this, individuals with PTSD often have sleep difficulties and angry outbursts. Men and women become mistrusting and may lash out at the world or harm themselves. They may self-medicate to help alleviate their symptoms, and they may become addicted. Parrots react similarly. They use their beaks and nails to protect themselves from threats, real or perceived. Parrots don't have access to drugs, so they turn to self-mutilation.

PTSD and other symptoms of trauma are not limited to humans. Indeed, other species often exploited by humans, such as chimpanzees and elephants, have been known to develop such disorders. Many if not most of the parrots coming to our sanctuary appeared to suffer the avian equivalent of PTSD.

I imagined this VA sanctuary as a means of resolving the psychological problems not only of the veterans but of the parrots. One way we could help the birds was restoring their sense of independence: they should be able to choose their own food, flockmates, and places to fly. Limited food choice can be a source of depression in animals in captivity, because foraging is a psychological imperative for them. I would make sure that an abundance of species-specific food was provided in a way that would require the parrots to seek it out. I would also ensure that every bird could interact with the flock while providing options for privacy. As we had done at the Ojai sanctuary, our birds would feel secure and be able to satisfy as many of the Four Fs as possible. A natural environment would help the birds slowly feel more comfortable and begin to work their way back to healing.

Similarly, veterans could heal in a tranquil environment with a minimum of triggering stimuli. The only loud noises would be natural ones. We'd develop a network of comrades who understood their shared experiences, a big brother / big sister system, or maybe even a "band of brothers." They would work to help others, bird and human, and they would be outdoors, not confined to an office with bright lights or a factory with artificial noises. They would be learning how to trust and how to earn the trust of others. I had seen hundreds of veterans at this point, quite a few struggling with PTSD. Many were receiving treatment, yet we were still losing too many. In the twenty years following the end of the Vietnam War, thousands of Vietnam veterans had ended their lives through suicide or drug and alcohol abuse.

Ida agreed. We needed to get this done, and the Vet's Garden was the perfect location. Next I had to get the necessary approvals. When we'd gone to the West Los Angeles VA years earlier to get New Directions started, we were told there were no homeless veterans. Things had changed. The VA knew homelessness was a real problem.

America had invaded Afghanistan in 2001 and would invade Iraq in 2003. Soldiers were beginning to trickle back with horrible wounds, both physical and mental, and the VA knew these men and women needed help.

As part of my work at New Directions, I had clinical meetings with all the departments at the VA: Nursing, Psychology, Psychiatry, Social Work, Infectious Disease, Physical Therapy, Occupational Therapy. I was talking to friends and colleagues, not strangers. I began sharing stories about Earth Angel Parrot Sanctuary at our meetings. Veterans were talking about how different, and how much better, they felt around the birds. I drew up a petition to bring parrot therapy to the VA, and, to my surprise, the heads of the various departments signed it.

Earl Gardner, a Vietnam veteran, had led PTSD groups at the VA for thirty years. Earl was an African American with dreadlocks who wore traditional clothes he'd picked up on his many trips to Africa. He helped many of the other African American veterans research their family roots. He always had a smile and a hug, and when I told him about the parrots, he nodded. "They talk, after all," he said. "And they're in cages, like many of our veterans are wrapped up in. I'll help you." I knew I had another ally.

I arranged a meeting with the medical director at the West Los Angeles VA campus and the managers of the Asset Management Department. We had worked together on starting the second program for veterans with dual diagnoses after the VA proposed it.

"It will not cost the VA a penny, and I will pull up that dilapidated old basketball court," I told them. "It's an eyesore and it's dangerous. I'll make it beautiful." They were listening, but I could tell from their faces that they needed to hear more.

"I will provide employment for veterans in perpetuity, with no cost to the VA. I will teach job skills so they can obtain permanent employment in careers, not just menial labor."

"It all sounds great, but we don't have the authority to approve it ourselves," the medical director said. "Talk to Charles Dorman."

The VA is a bureaucracy. In an organization as large as the VA, that can be a good thing, providing checks and balances to limit any one person's power. It also meant, however, that even armed with a petition, even with the support of department directors and people such as Earl Gardner, it wasn't a simple matter to approve the sanctuary.

Charles was CEO of the West Los Angeles VA at the time. He approved of New Directions' mission and was happy with my work. I explained to him how the parrots could provide an innovative therapy. Some hospitals, such as Walter Reed National Military Medical Center, in Maryland, were under fire for poor care of veterans. Unsanitary conditions, long waits, and insufficient treatment were too common. The hospital was accused of neglecting the men and women who gave their bodies and their minds for this country. The VA hospital in West Los Angeles had its own problems. The parrot sanctuary offered Charles the opportunity for productive change. He was willing to take a chance on innovation.

With Charles behind me, I was able to move forward. The VA trusted that I would carry through on my commitment to build a place where veterans could learn valuable job skills. We had a location at the Vet's Garden. But I still needed to get architectural and engineering plans and then have them approved through two critical departments: Engineering and Building and Safety. I was going to have to raise the money for that myself.

They say you should be able to deliver your idea in the time it takes to ride an elevator. I didn't understand that maxim until I ended up delivering a remarkably literal elevator pitch.

One day, while I was attending a conference at UCLA, I was riding in an elevator where I heard a man discussing the course he was teaching in architecture.

"Are you an architect?" I asked, after apologizing for interrupting his conversation.

He was. I told him my dilemma. I needed complicated architectural and engineering plans, but I had very little money. As the elevator doors opened, he said, "I'll do it." That was how I met Rouben Mohiuddin, who had studied under Frank Gehry. Rouben was a successful architect who had worked on dozens of commercial and residential projects, but he also took time to contribute his skills to the community.

Rouben refused to take a penny and even introduced me to the head of one of LA's top engineering firms. He agreed to do the work at cost. Rouben's students provided much of the labor as community service. People really liked the idea of this program for parrots and vets!

But cage wire is extremely expensive (because zinc is toxic to birds, we have to buy special wire not containing or coated with that metal) and so is laying concrete. Plus, I'd made a promise to employ veterans. Even with all those generous people helping us, we'd still need a lot of cash. I knew if we had a substantial part of the money, other people would be more willing to contribute. No one wants to write a check for something that's never going to get accomplished. I needed a big donor, so I went to see my old friend Al Jacobson.

Al was a wealthy entrepreneur, but I'd met him when he was just starting out. When I was still a student at UCLA, he had hired me to make deliveries in my ratty old van. Al could sell anything. He once was a door-to-door salesman of vacuum cleaners and encyclopedias—at the same time. Then, while attending a food expo, he saw a need for whole-wheat pita bread. He walked around the expo talking about the wonders of whole wheat, and he took orders. He didn't let a little thing—like not actually having a source of whole-wheat pitas—stop him.

Al found a Lebanese baker. The man's products were made with care, and Al liked that.

"Pitas aren't made with whole wheat," the baker said.

"Have you tried?"

"Of course not," the baker said. "I make them the right way. Whole wheat we feed to the pigs."

"I'm just asking you to give this a chance," Al said.

The baker shrugged. "I'll make them for you, but no one will buy them."

People did buy them, though. Al understood that people wanted a healthier version of a traditional food, and he made it happen. He loved discovering trends, finding a need and filling it, talking to strangers and selling them something they wanted, even if they didn't know it yet.

His biggest success was blue-corn tortillas chips. Who knew that people wanted something like that before he started selling them? Before Al popularized it, blue corn was used mostly as animal feed. Al decided to take a chance. "I'll take your whole crop," he told a farmer in New Mexico.

Al was a born salesman, and his product was health. He would frequently say, "I have a vision," and it was always something hopeful and positive; I never heard him say a negative word about anyone in all the years I knew him. "We're going to bring healthy food to everyone," he said. He wasn't in business just to make money. He wanted people to eat their way to health.

Garden of Eatin', he called his company. Back when I first knew him, it was little more than an idea. Now blue-corn chips, and especially Garden of Eatin's, are everywhere. The idea of healthy eating has spread across the country. People now understand the benefits of whole, minimally processed food. Al had a lot to do with that.

Al actually cared about people and it was a pleasure working for him. It also helped me pay for UCLA, but I didn't work with him just for the money. We were friends, and we remained friends for the rest of his life. He had come a long way from begging a Lebanese baker to fill his orders. True to his nature, he gave donations to numerous environmental and health causes. He cared about making the world a better place.

"Al," I said, "so many parrots are in need. They are homeless just like the veterans I care for. The sanctuary can help them both."

"Magical. It will be like feeding two birds with the same food," said my peace-loving, dear old friend. He'd never think of saying "killing two birds with one stone."

Al's love of natural living wasn't limited to food. He preferred a natural approach to medical and psychiatric treatment as well. Al had lived through the years when lobotomies and electroconvulsive therapy were routinely performed and ravaged lives. He saw my program as a non-traditional way to help heal souls, and he respected that. I had introduced him to Sammy and Mango, and he found them to be "angels of this earth."

He donated more than half the money we needed to get started.

We raised the rest from other donors; it was easier now that we could tell them about Al's donation. The task had seemed impossible, but an old friend's help started us on our way. The parrots and the veterans were ready to start making miracles happen.

* * *

As I had feared, it took years for Serenity Park to finally get all the necessary permits. We finally broke ground in 2004.

A group of ten of us drove up to the old, dilapidated basketball courts. With me were Rouben Mohiuddin, the architect who helped us so much on our journey, as well as Miriam Harasti and Joanna Sinclair, his students. Bruce Rosen, a board member of Friends of the Garden, was there as well. Other parrot and nature lovers rounded out our group.

There was nothing there but broken asphalt and weeds, but it was a quiet place shaded by tall, old ficus trees. The Vet's Garden bordered the basketball courts, and we could see the squash vines spreading out from the garden plots and smell the basil warming in the sun. Everyone laughed and talked as we pulled our tools from the trucks. I wrapped my hand around the wooden handle of a pickax and swung. I enjoyed the solid, satisfying sound of breaking asphalt. I could feel the force vibrating up my arms. I smiled. Finally.

We used large machinery to do a lot of the demolition

work and to prepare the area for the foundations, but, at least at the beginning, we wanted to get our hands dirty. It felt good to begin the physical labor of clearing the land.

By then, I had resigned from New Directions. I believed in the program, and I still do. But while the people at New Directions were doing everything in their power to help veterans stay clean, doctors were still prescribing Vicodin to the same veterans: opiates for veterans struggling with addiction at a residential drug and alcohol rehabilitation program! This happened time and again, not for major trauma but for simple things like headaches, toothaches, and backaches. Over-the-counter painkillers would have addressed these problems, and they would have done so without the risk of addiction. Fortunately, most of our veterans were working hard to stay clean and sober, and they handed all of these painkillers to our Medication Take Back Department to be disposed of properly. On top of that, while the veterans had no problem getting medication, they were not getting the treatments that would help resolve the underlying problems. The VA was underfunded and understaffed, and veterans waited days or even months to see specialists.

I left New Directions to pursue going to medical school so that I could solve these problems from the inside. I got part of the way toward that goal but life got in the way, and instead of medical school I ended up creating a new mental health treatment model for veterans—parrot therapy at the VA.

* * *

Serenity Park had a promising beginning, but there was tremendous sorrow, too. Just days before I was going to pick up Sammy and Mango from the Ojai sanctuary and bring them to the new sanctuary at the VA, I received a frantic call from the caretaker there. She had found Mango on the ground, bleeding.

During traumatic incidents, we often enter a dissociated state. Everything seems surreal. People sometimes describe a sense of time moving slowly or feeling outside of their bodies and watching their movements from above. I can't recall the drive to Ojai to pick up Mango. A friend drove, and I held Mango in my arms from the moment we got to the sanctuary until he was at the veterinarian's office. He was struggling to breathe, slowly opening and closing his eyes. There was so much blood I couldn't tell where his wounds were. His eyes were dull and glazed. It was Labor Day weekend, and my avian veterinarian was out of town. I brought Mango to a twenty-four-hour veterinary hospital, and I stayed with him all night.

The veterinarian bandaged his wounds and stopped the bleeding. He gave him fluids. Without blood everywhere, Mango looked more like himself.

He slept some, and I leaned close to make sure he was still breathing. I watched his little chest rise and fall. "Please, hold on," I said.

When he woke up, he managed to maintain eye contact. His breath was ragged but steady. He seemed to be feeling better. I ran next door to an all-night restaurant and bought a baked sweet potato. He swallowed a few bites. Maybe he'd make it, I thought. He was a tough little guy.

He didn't stay conscious for long. Each time he slept, I silently begged him to wake up again.

But the next morning, he took his last breath. His little body shuddered, and he was gone.

The veterinarian on duty said there had been just too much trauma.

He had been attacked by a raccoon. We had built secure aviaries not just to keep the birds in but also to keep predators out. Raccoons are smart, and they got around our protections. They watched the birds and figured out that if they grabbed and shook the wire mesh of an aviary, a bird might fly or fall to the ground. As the bird climbed back up to his perch, the raccoon could reach through the cage wire and grab his foot. The parrots learned to avoid the raccoons by flying straight back to their perch. But Mango couldn't fly. He had to climb up the side of the enclosure.

Maybe he was curious about the raccoons. Mango was always curious about others. Maybe he even said a final "Hewwo."

Mango couldn't be gone. How could it be a beautiful, ordinary California day without him here? I still had his blood on me, dried on my shirt. I was shaking, whether from exhaustion or grief, I couldn't tell. I loved that bird. He'd made me and everyone around him laugh. He was full of affection and compassion and loyalty.

I wish I'd built that aviary in Ojai the way I was building them at Serenity Park, with the cage wire only a quarter-inch wide so no little raccoon paws could fit through. I wish I had taken Mango back to Los Angeles the weekend before. But all of that wishing was in vain.

I cried. I slept more than usual. Sometimes I just stared into space, thinking of the things I could have done differently. Sometimes I felt weighed down, detached from the world moving on around me. I had not been so devastated since my mother died. My little man was gone.

I'd lost more than a parrot. I know that now. As a psychologist, I realize that one loss can compound past losses. A snowball gains mass and momentum as it rolls downhill, and so does pain. I knew that some of my grief, which seemed inconsolable, was for others I had lost and not fully mourned. I had tried to bury the pain. Denial can seem so useful at times, but as Bessel van der Kolk, one of the leading researchers in traumatic stress, states, "The body keeps the score." Grief always remains in us, somewhere in our bodies and minds.

I can write about this now because I did have the opportunity to work through my losses. I missed my mother. I wished I had had a happier childhood with a mother who wasn't ill. I missed the friends I'd lost through the years. I felt alone. Mango's death spurred me into starting psychoanalysis, and that allowed me to forgive myself, the raccoons, and anyone else I'd wanted to blame to make my grief easier in the moment.

One thing I still felt awful about was that Sammy must have been terrified. For the first time, I was glad that she and Mango hadn't formed a mated pair and so she didn't have to mourn as deeply. I drove back to Earth Angel Parrot Sanctuary in Ojai early on the morning Mango died and brought Sammy home with me. She was jumpy and agitated, but in a few days she was calmer. She didn't enter a period of deep mourning. I couldn't ask her if she missed Mango, though I suspect she did, but it was a friend she was missing, not her partner.

I cried every night for weeks. I kept Sammy with me for a long time, even though Serenity Park was now up and running. I just couldn't let her go again.

I still think about Mango nearly every day, but I would never exchange the pain of losing him for never having known him. His absence on this planet does not mean my love for him is diminished. There is a little place in my heart where sunshine can no longer reach, but that doesn't mean I won't seize every opportunity for love. When I think of Mango, I think of this quote by Khalil Gibran:

> When you are sorrowful look again in your heart, and you shall see that in truth you are weeping for that which has been your delight.

SEVEN

A Sailor's Story

The purpose of life is not to be happy—but to matter, to be productive, to be useful, to have it make some difference that you have lived at all.

—LEO ROSTEN, screenwriter, author, and political scientist

To understand the need for a place like Serenity Park, it helps to understand veterans and PTSD. That comprehension cannot be found in a diagnostic manual. Humans are far too complex to be defined by a set of diagnostic criteria.

When I taught Abnormal Psychology, I told my students that we never call someone by his or her diagnosis. "There goes that schizophrenic" and "Your bipolar patient is here" aren't phrases any psychotherapist should ever utter.

There's judgment in those phrases, and psychotherapists, of all people, should understand that a diagnosis is not a person, nor is it a source of shame. Why does the brain get blamed for things it can't help? When we have biochemical disorders like diabetes, we don't say, "Shame on that pancreas!" People who have schizophrenia or bipolar disorder also have biochemical disorders; it just happens that those disorders are in the brain instead of the endocrine system. The human mind is influenced by a combination of genetics, the environment, and all the things any individual has experienced, starting in utero. A person is never just someone with PTSD; he or she is a complex sum of all his or her experiences.

Matt Simmons is one such person. Matt grew up in Cincinnati, Ohio, in an affluent area filled with country clubs. His parents sent him to private schools. Matt lived his entire childhood in the same sprawling, well-appointed house surrounded by trees. His father was a prominent attorney. Matt's mother, too, was successful, not only as a nurse practitioner but also as a dedicated community member helping pregnant teens. She did her work while raising a son and two daughters. Matt was the eldest.

From the outside, it seemed that Matt's childhood was happy and predictable. Matt's parents had a close relationship, and they were observant Catholics who went to church every Sunday. In addition, Matt was close to his grandfather, a loving man and excellent role model. Matt's reality, though, was not as idyllic as it appeared.

Matt's father served in the Vietnam War as an interpreter. He rarely discussed the war. As a translator, he would have sat in on interrogations, and he may have been exposed to brutality. Matt believes he never sat with his back to the door. He thought he was too quick to anger. His father once told Matt that if he ever jumped out of a helicopter, he'd better make damn sure he was running downhill. He never explained what was behind that advice, but Matt knew it wasn't a story with a nice ending. Matt suspected his father might have suffered some emotional wounds in the war but he couldn't be sure because, to his knowledge, his father never complained or sought help. What Matt feels sure of is that his father would never hug him. Hugs were for sissies.

Matt is the type of person who will say what's on his mind, whether it's sarcastic or kind. If he's unhappy with the work someone is doing, he's not afraid to bark out orders, just as he's not afraid to pat someone on the back. He likes to joke around, and he is very playful, so you often do not know if he is being serious. I can imagine him acting the same way with his father, the high-powered lawyer who wanted compliance and conformity. Matt always had questions. Matt perceived a lack of warmth from his parents, though he admits some of his parents' coldness came because he was such a cheeky and defiant child. Regardless, there was no physical affection, no words of praise in his household—not for him, anyway. Despite appearing so independent from an early age, he actually needed more emotional support, not less. The coldness made him hurt inside, and that hurt turned to anger.

He believed fists were the answer to his problems. When he was about twelve, he had a girlfriend whose cousin was gay. Bullies locked the boy in a locker and peed on him. The next day, Matt skipped school and found the kids. He broke one boy's arm and kicked another down the stairs. Looking back as an adult, Matt regrets hurting the boys, but, at the time, using his fists felt natural. It didn't even occur to him that he could have talked it out, that he could have gone to the principal for advice. It was a violent act, but Matt saw it as a way of helping his girlfriend and her cousin, of expressing caring for a victim.

Matt was attracted to danger. From BASE jumping, to riding motorcycles too fast, to experimenting with drugs and alcohol: he loved the excitement of it all. It wasn't that he wanted to hurt himself; he just needed some kind of rush or some kind of oblivion.

Matt's parents sent him to a boys' parochial school. He made good grades without trying, but his list of black marks kept getting longer: wrecking a car, bad language, and, always, violence. The school didn't help to curb these tendencies. They'd lace up the boys' fists in boxing gloves and throw them into the ring to solve their problems. When he was seventeen, a boy he was boxing was sent to the hospital, and the school finally kicked Matt out.

After he was expelled, his parents sent him to the local public school. When the principal and counselor saw his record, they asked to meet with him. They were going to read him the riot act. Instead, Matt imposed his own conditions. "Look," he said, "I've only got a few credits to graduate. If you leave me alone, I promise I'll ace every class. If you try to make me come every day, that won't happen."

They worked something out. Even as a bratty teenager, Matt must have been convincing. They weren't about to let him skip school, of course, so he agreed to pass all his exams if they allowed him to do a work-study program. Matt's neighbor was a well-known painter whose work had appeared on the cover of *Rolling Stone*. Instead of being confined to a classroom, Matt spent six hours a day interning with him.

Matt did his own art, mostly painting and drawing, and he was good at it. His first painting was of a pit bull wearing a Brooks Brothers suit. He called it *Lawyer*. Not surprisingly his father wasn't amused.

Matt kept his word. He graduated, but his father wasn't willing to pay for him to study art in college. Artists don't often make a lot of money, and Matt's father didn't think it was wise to pay for an education that didn't provide for a livelihood. Since there aren't many student-aid programs for children from wealthy families, Matt wasn't able to pay for school.

He had to find another path. His grades were good, and he was strong and healthy. He had grown up on John Wayne movies, and he believed in the fundamental goodness of America and its military. He had no problem with aggression, and he certainly wasn't lacking in courage, or at least the willingness to take risks. He enlisted in the navy.

He found a program where he could serve two years as an enlisted man, spend four years in ROTC in college, and then become a commissioned officer. When he took the entrance exam, he scored in the top 1 percent. With that score, the navy allowed him to pick his first job.

The navy had a giant book, as large as a big-city white pages, listing each job available. He flipped through it. Each one entailed dangers. There was no war at the time, but Matt didn't want to be on the front lines if that happened. Risk-taking was a way of making life bearable, not ending it.

He picked yeoman. He'd have to keep records like a secretary. People who keep records, he thought, don't get shot at. People who keep records stay nice and safe on the ship.

Matt chose an F-18 fighter squadron for his deployment, so he expected he'd be stationed on an aircraft carrier. If the navy kept anything safe, it would be an aircraft carrier. Besides, it was the spring of 1990. America hadn't been in a large military conflict since the Vietnam War. Matt signed up, and he prepared for two uneventful and safe years.

He couldn't have been more wrong.

* * *

A few weeks before he left, Matt married his high school sweetheart. Matt had a feeling he would not be coming back, though he wasn't sure why. If he died, he wanted to leave a family behind. He had known his wife since grade school, so even if it wasn't the greatest romance, it felt like a natural next step to Matt.

Saddam Hussein invaded Kuwait in August of 1990. Matt wasn't worried. Iraq wasn't a world power; it would back down soon under international pressure. When the United Nations Security Council approved the use of force in November, Matt realized combat might be a reality. He was glad to fight for his country, but he was also glad he wasn't going to be on the front lines.

In training, his commanders yelled at him every day. He'd be asked to jog at one in the morning, holding a rifle above his head. If he lowered his arms, he got yelled at. If he fell down, he got yelled at. The recruits crawled in the mud. If they lifted themselves too high, they got yelled at.

Matt didn't like it, but he was used to being disciplined. He was smart, tough, and fast. His superiors noticed that he followed orders and could handle anything they threw at him. He was appointed the recruit chief petty officer. As the RCPO, he was responsible for maintaining order in his division, keeping an eye on things when higher-ups weren't around.

By the time Matt graduated from his training program, the United States was launching an invasion, but no one told the soldiers this when their ship sailed from Norfolk, Virginia. The enlisted men thought they were heading to Puerto Rico. Matt planned to do his work, keep his head down, and maybe sneak a little Puerto Rican rum. As they left the harbor, Matt noticed the sun setting behind him to the west. They were going in the wrong direction.

"Sir," he said to an officer, "if we're going to Puerto Rico, shouldn't the sun be over there?"

"Good eye," the officer answered. "You're headed to the Persian Gulf."

Before they arrived, Saddam Hussein set fire to most of the oil wells. He wanted to keep the United States from getting the oil. He also knew that all those burning wells would create a massive cloud of smoke and debris. Bombers wouldn't be able to see, and what they couldn't see, they couldn't hit. With the heat of the fires, the Americans couldn't rely on heat-seeking missiles to find what their eyes could not.

The military still planned to hit Saddam Hussein, and since it had to have a record—the military is all about records—the yeomen had to go out on the ground.

Matt was one of two yeomen on his ship. They worked in shifts, twelve hours in country, twelve hours back on ship. They were escorted by a group of marines. One of the first rules you learn in the military is to never give your gun to anybody. When Matt and the marines went out the first time, the lead marine barked an order for Matt to hand over his weapon. Matt knew the rules, but he also knew that the man standing in front of him was serious. These guys were responsible for his life, so he gave up his gun. The marine emptied the cartridge and handed it back.

"When you're with us, you never pull a gun. You never do anything but follow."

The marine nodded toward one of his men. "See that?" he asked Matt, pointing to a plastic handle on the soldier's back. It looked like a suitcase handle the marines had sewed on themselves. They probably had. "Your job is to hold that and keep your head down. Nothing else. Got it?"

He got it.

When they left, Matt's commanding officer said to his escort, "If Simmons is killed, bring back his notebooks."

Matt spent the rest of the war huddled in a cluster of marines, recording hits, marking targets. He was surrounded by the destruction wrought by the Americans and the impact on those who survived. He kept his head down as ordered, but he saw and heard everything on the ground. No matter where they went, it was the same. Rubble. Smoke. Blackened bodies forever caught in the moment of crawling away from the flames. The smell of dust and burning flesh overlaid with the thick stench of oil.

He went to the site of bomb strikes to record the damage. Nothing was left but dust. Wherever he went in Iraq, he was breathing in broken buildings and broken bodies.

He was told to stop shaving and keep bathing to a minimum. To do nothing to stand out and make himself a target. Above all else, to keep those notebooks safe. He ran, ducked, and scribbled.

He never fired a shot, but he was shot at plenty.

When he was back at sea, he discovered that an aircraft carrier during wartime wasn't the safe haven he had envisioned. There was unending noise and activity. Steam-pressured catapults helped cutting-edge fighter jets blast into the air. Those same jets landed on the tightest of runways. It felt like standing on a six-lane freeway at dusk, and the men and women on deck were charged with putting hood orna-ments on the passing cars. The slightest misstep could get you or your fellow sailors killed, and everyone had to work faster than they could think. Jet engines could suck people in or blast them into the sea. People were hurt even without the enemy firing on them. One pilot had an accident while landing. He saw her helmet, with her head still inside, float-ing in the water.

He also came to understand that John Wayne movies have nothing to do with modern warfare. Matt had seen foot-age of soldiers in World War II handing out candy to Ger-man children. But the marines shot anything that came over the horizon. They attacked first and figured out whether it was their intended target later. The soldiers on the ground were never sure whether the people they encountered were civilians or military, and, if they were civilians, they still weren't sure where their loyalties lay. They didn't want people to flee and bring back reinforcements.

It sure didn't feel to Matt as if the United States was pro-tecting the people of Kuwait and Iraq from an oppressive Iraqi dictator. It felt as if the United States was the enemy.

* * *

When the war was over, Matt came home. His life didn't fall apart. He was married, he enrolled in college, he played sports, and he taught himself about computers. He liked writ-ing code. There were no emotions involved, and he controlled each line. He got really good at it. He appeared to be a man with a limitless future, at least from the outside.

On the inside, though, Matt was pulled tight. He had the symptoms of PTSD, but he made excuses for the anger and the fear. He was working too hard. He was experiencing stress at home. He certainly wasn't one of those weaklings who got back from war and fell apart. It seemed to him, and probably to those around him, that he was acting like a man, stoic and aloof.

Matt and his wife had a son, born prematurely. They adored their baby. Matt spent weeks in the neonatal unit with his son. When the baby came home from the hospital, Matt's wife spent all her time taking care of their tiny child. Matt worked to support his family; he believed in the old-fashioned way of doing things, as he'd learned from his grandfather. That meant hours away from his family so he could create a future for the three of them.

But the wounds from the war were catching up with him. Soon after he came home, he started having nightmares. Three years later, his dreams had progressed to night terrors. He'd wake up sweating, heart racing, ready to flee. He was always a moment away from exploding with rage. He was worried he'd hurt someone.

Matt shut himself off even from those close to him. He and his wife didn't discuss his feelings. He didn't feel comfortable joining his college classmates at parties or even in study groups. He was always on guard, never entering a room without knowing an escape route. In a lecture or at a restaurant, he'd always sit nearest the exit, never with his back to the door.

Five years after returning from combat, there was a

never-ending tape playing in his head. He saw the destruction, the smell and sight of death in Iraq, day and night. He trusted no one unless he knew them well. He wasn't sleeping. He had to take Ambien and wash it down with wine to get any rest at all. He unconsciously avoided triggers, such as loud noises or flashing lights. He couldn't watch anything about the war in Iraq and Afghanistan, whether on the news or fictionalized.

He didn't want to be an artist anymore. That desire was gone. He wasn't drawn to anything he studied. Mostly, he looked forward to the hour when he could start drinking.

Maybe Dad was right, he thought. Maybe he should just become a lawyer. At least he'd support his family financially. It seemed like the path of least resistance.

He decided to study for the LSAT. At his father's law firm, he sat in a room filled with books and worked. He was buddies with one of his father's partners. Matt was bored and he liked to talk. He asked his friend: "All these books, how do you know what's in them?"

"That's why we go to law school."

"Say I want to look up, I don't know, cases based on federal drug laws. How would I do that?"

"I'm not that type of lawyer, Matt."

"But you are a lawyer. How would you do it?"

His friend explained. Suffice it to say that he didn't just go to a card catalog or computer and look up "cocaine." He'd follow a chain of cases, seeing where they'd been cited by other courts, then he'd follow those cases. It took hours just to see if a statute or a legal precedent was still good law. It made for a lot of expensive legal libraries and billable hours, but it didn't make any sense.

"What if you could just look it up on a computer?" Matt asked.

Matt was an expert on computers. He had access to an extensive legal library. It turned out there was a legal tech service, a lawyer version of Google, that allowed lawyers to look up cases, but it wasn't easily searchable. You couldn't just type in a few key words and get the most relevant cases. You could do it, though, Matt thought, if someone built a good, searchable database.

Matt realized he'd stumbled upon something big. He was going to build a case-law database. He'd hire people to read, summarize, and highlight key words for cases. He found a partner to team up with. Money wasn't hard to get. It was 1994, and if you had a computer company, "you could get money by writing a business proposal on a napkin," Matt joked.

He and his partner started building their database, but it wasn't long before he realized his company was researching only a small section of the law. The small firms he did business with were interested in DUIs, drunk and disorderlies, family law: searches that were easy to do and easy to replicate. Instead of creating a huge, searchable legal library, Matt and his partner were in the business of selling a few easily replicable searches. They started operating in other states, and they were growing every day.

Matt was still drinking heavily, and he was taking other drugs as well. Work kept him busy, though, so he had some check on his substance abuse.

The legal tech service guys saw Matt as competition, and soon they began making accusations of copyright infringement. "Take money from us for a buyout," they demanded.

Matt's partner thought they should take the offer, but Matt wanted to fight. In 2001, the Napster decision came down, and Matt realized they weren't going to win a fight over copyright infringement. He sat down with representatives from the firm and a bunch of lawyers from both sides. They slid an envelope across the desk.

"We're buying your company," they said. "Here's our offer."

Matt accepted the deal. He took the money and signed a noncompete clause, agreeing to stay on retainer. Now Matt had more money than he could spend and hardly any work to keep him busy.

He had begun drinking earlier in the day. He found doctors who were more than willing to write prescriptions for painkillers. He'd come into the office in the morning, play a round of golf, and have a long, liquid lunch. By afternoon, he'd switch over to other drugs, and he wouldn't stop until he passed out.

His wife asked him to quit. She needed him, she said, and so did his son who had grown into a bright and loving child. Matt did quit, for a day or two at a time. Then he'd stay out all night. He knew he was hurting his family by not coming home, but, in his own way, he was trying to protect them. He believed there was an addictive gene in his family, so he didn't want his son to see him drunk or high. "I'd do anything for my son," Matt claimed, "and somehow I thought this was the right thing to do at the time."

Soon his wife was gone, and so was his son. Matt's addiction drove them away.

Still, he was clean and sober when he visited his son. At the end of one visit, though, he began to go into withdrawal, sweating and shaking. "Daddy is feeling sick," his son said to his mother when it was time for drop-off. Matt realized how serious the problem had become, and he never wanted to expose his son to that again. He quit cold turkey. But a week later, on his next scheduled visit with his son, he found himself driving to his dealer's house instead of his child's. The old patterns sidelined him. He'd struggled, sick with withdrawal for an entire week, yet he was about to throw everything away to get high.

I can't do this to my son, he thought. He got back into the car and drove. He didn't stop until he was across the country. When he reached Santa Barbara, he checked into a rehab program. The doctor at the clinic diagnosed Matt with PTSD. He wanted to put him on medication. Matt didn't want meds. Relying on drugs had torn his life apart.

Matt hated himself. His parents hated him as well; they told him he was a moral failure who'd destroyed his family. He thought of his grandfather, a strong, loving man who'd always put others first, and he felt selfish and weak. He let his wife and son keep all the family's money and cut ties with them. It's better for them, he thought, than having me around.

He graduated from rehab, but he didn't stay clean long, and one time, while he was out drinking, he got into a fight. The other guy swung first, but Matt had boxing experience. He hit the guy twice and knocked him out. It was Matt's first adult offense, but the district attorney sought a long prison sentence. The person he'd fought was an off-duty police officer. Matt was placed in a jail gang unit, and he sat in a six-by-eight-foot cell twenty-three hours a day.

For two years, he fought to avoid being sent to prison, and he fought to stay sober. When he'd cleaned up previously, he hadn't been truly dedicated to sobriety. Now he knew he had to get clean or die.

He didn't get a lot out of sitting in groups talking, but he did read *The Big Book of Alcoholics Anonymous* cover to cover. He threw himself into recovery the way he'd thrown himself into everything in his life. He vowed never to take a drug, any drug, again.

Matt was able to avoid prison because he was a veteran; an advocate from a veteran-based program at the West Los Angeles VA dropped a card into his jail cell. "Call me when you get out" was all he said. When he got out of jail, Matt called and went straight to that program.

That program was New Directions. I had left three years before and was now down the hill at Serenity Park.

New Directions was run military-style. Up at 5 a.m., calisthenics, marching, uniforms, six bunks to a room, a mess hall: this structure was familiar to Matt and he felt comfortable. He wasn't nearly as comfortable with the group therapy at New Directions or the PTSD groups at the VA that he was required to attend.

He went to therapy but wouldn't talk about anything important. His PTSD groups were a bunch of guys from the Vietnam War who talked about "Charlie" and being in the jungle. They were older than he was. No one was discussing the war he knew. He crossed his arms and ticked off the minutes until he could walk out. He saw many veterans in those groups who looked like they were over-drugged on prescription medications, zombielike. That was not going to be him. Why substitute one drug for another?

Then John Keaveney, the man who'd founded New Directions, noticed Matt. John told Matt he saw potential in him and took him under his wing. Matt felt closer to John than he had to anyone in a long time. Like Matt, John threw himself into his interests with a passionate intensity. Like Matt, he'd gone to serve his country and ended up addicted to drugs. Like Matt, John was an intelligent person who had made foolish choices, a problem kid who wanted to change his ways. Like Matt, John could be temperamental and even verbally abusive, but he'd also vowed to change. His friendship with John allowed Matt to understand the benefits of therapy. John helped him see that working the Twelve Step Program was going to be what saved him and he knew that he had to make amends to those he'd hurt.

As Matt got more in touch with giving back and being of service, he was better able to "hear" his therapist and better able to forgive. His therapist suggested he try volunteering at the parrot sanctuary. "Don't worry," he told Matt, "it's not in the hospital, or any building, for that matter, it's down-campus where there aren't any therapists looking to shrink your head."

Matt was a city kid from the Midwest. For all he knew parrots were no different from chickens. What would he be doing? Whatever it was, he figured it would be better than being trapped inside all day. He could throw a little feed on the ground and sweep up. He agreed to give it a try.

Matt had arrived at Serenity Park. That's where he met Ruby. That's where his life changed forever.

EIGHT

A Sanctuary Opens at the VA

Digging in the soil has a curative effect on the
mentally ill.

—Dr. Benjamin Rush, signer of the
Declaration of Independence

Serenity Park finally opened its aviary doors in 2005. The
sanctuary looks more like a garden than like a typical animal shelter. Though it's neat and orderly—the entrance leads
to two aisles, each flanked by rows of large enclosures—it's
also purposefully rustic. Benches and chairs are scattered
about, seemingly at random. Flower and plant beds decorate
the grounds. There's a small building with a kitchen for preparing food and room for storage, but mostly you see the sky.
Wood chips are a relatively inexpensive and low-maintenance
solution for the walkways, but they also soften sounds and
give the whole place a gentle, natural smell.

Serenity Park is peaceful. Before the birds notice you, all
you hear are muted footsteps as you walk under the embrac-
ing shade of giant eucalyptus trees. Yet to get here, you have

to drive through the densest traffic in the city of Los Angeles and one of the world's busiest intersections, Wilshire and Sepulveda. When you turn in to the West Los Angeles VA Medical Center, you follow winding roads, first bustling with health-care professionals and patients, then quieter as you make your way through the nearly four-hundred-acre campus. You pass an elaborate clapboard chapel and a street car depot built in the 1890s. When this facility first got its start, combat veterans from the Civil War walked hundreds of miles to Los Angeles to see this land dedicated for them as the Pacific Branch of the National Home for Disabled Volunteer Soldiers. This facility is now the site of one of the country's largest veterans' hospitals and home to one of the largest veteran populations.

Serenity Park sits at the lowest point on the grounds, far from the busy city, as its name implies. Gentle sunlight filters through the copses of ficus and plum trees, and the luxuriant purple sand verbena, fragrant pitcher sage, and winecup flowers are tantalizing to every sense. You don't feel as if you are in a city at all, even though you are surrounded by some of the most valuable real estate in this country.

Arriving at the sanctuary is magical. Every time I walk in, I feel the calmness and joy present here. This is my version of healing: being connected to the natural world. At Serenity Park those heroes who have been seeking a road home are offered a map to help them get there.

The aviaries are made of wire mesh, and the parrots can see the trees, the veterans, and the birds in the other enclosures. A few birds are alone in their aviaries, but most live with other birds; we respect their need for companionship as well as for privacy. Even the parrots in individual enclosures can see or hear the rest of the flock; they are never isolated.

As I walk into the sanctuary, I see Stevie, an outgoing umbrella cockatoo, in the first aviary by the entrance. He's a pure white bird, and when he raises his crest—a great, ruffled fan larger than his head—it suits his demonstrative personality. "Hello, sweetheart!" he calls out warmly. I offer a quick hello, but there's someone I have to see first.

Unfailingly, clinging to the bars of the cage, with eyes wide in anticipation, there she is: Sammy, my dearest cockatoo. She calls to me.

"Hello are you!"

And then all hell breaks loose.

They've all spotted me now. Stevie, still trying to entice me to enter his aviary before anyone else's, repeats "Hello, sweetheart" dozens of times in the same high-pitched woman's voice. He sounds just like the woman who called me six years ago, desperate because her boyfriend told her it was him or the bird. Molly is doing her cappuccino-machine impersonation at a staccato pace, obviously having lived near someone's kitchen. Later it might be the *ding* of a microwave, repeated not once or twice but hundreds of times. Julius is singing like an opera star several octaves too high, his song interspersed with conversational Korean. Not to be outdone, Sunshine goes into an elaborate display. Stretching his wings to the fullest and bending his head forward, he lets out a mating call that would surely attract any female citron cockatoo for miles around. Others—and there are several dozen parrots of different species—join in the cacophony. It's pretty clear why so many parrots are given up. Their squawking can measure 130 decibels (jet engines measure 140).

Then, as if a switch has been flipped, the birds are quiet again. They have become accustomed to my presence. They may talk to each other in their own language, and sometimes in ours, calling out in a gregarious way, but the overwhelming din is gone. The parrots are eating, grooming one another, and freely flying around their aviaries. They are busy. They're just being parrots.

A sign welcomes veterans to the sanctuary, but other than that, very few people are aware of this oasis. It is outside of the conventional brick-and-mortar office setting where the mainstream "medical model" of healing commonly takes place at the VA.

Soon after I arrive, Matt Simmons walks in. He hasn't missed a day since his therapist sent him here from New Directions. Others trickle in later. First, they inspect the enclosures. Parrots are intelligent enough to plan mischief and dexterous and strong enough to carry it out. We need to find any damage and get it repaired. Next comes cleaning and feeding. The veterans spray down and sweep the cages, and, if they aren't spotless after inspection, they do it again. Cleanliness is crucial to preventing disease. The veterans chop fruits and vegetables for forage trays. They hide seeds and treats in the enclosures. They cook porridge and crack nuts for birds with injuries, such as crooked beaks. They administer whatever medicines and treatments the veterinarians have prescribed. We have our share of elderly and injured birds who need special attention.

When the regular work is finished, there's always something else to do. Maybe the generator needs fixing. Maybe we need to get started on a new enclosure. Maybe the flower beds need weeding and mulching. The veterans collect the large sticks the birds like to demolish. We often receive food deliveries and donations, and we need to sort out what the birds will use and what we'll pass on to other animal sanctuaries and rescue groups.

When they are done, the veterans take time to visit. They talk to their favorite birds. They laugh as the performers try to get their attention (Julius, for one, never seems to quiet down). Or they just sit quietly, petting a bird and enjoying being outdoors in the fresh air.

The veterans have been wounded, physically and mentally, but here they have resumed their roles of being of service by helping the birds. Some keep their heads down, not making eye contact or talking. Others, further along in their treatment, will smile and call out a hearty hello.

Sometimes you can hear the veterans joking with each other, with that familiar camaraderie found only among service members. Other times they are silent, focusing on their work or just enjoying the tranquility so hard to find elsewhere. When they enter the aviaries, they speak to the birds, stroke them, or let them perch on shoulders or arms. It's a safe place for them, and you can feel that.

It didn't take long for all our aviaries to fill up. People still call, and probably always will, because of the many reasons people can't keep parrots for their mutual lifetimes. We have been expanding since we've opened, but there's always more demand than we can ever meet.

"I'd like to donate my parrot to your program; the veterans will love her; when can I drop her off?" I've heard this appeal thousands of times.

"I'm so sorry but we're full," I have to say most of the

time. I've referred people to other sanctuaries around the country, but they are relatively few and filling up, too.

Birds were easy, too easy, to find. It was the veterans I was having a harder time attracting. I had a handful of volunteers, but I still hadn't found a real employee, someone who made a connection with the birds and wanted to stick around.

I also needed to fully develop what the concept of "work therapy" would be for the veterans since they would be paid for their involvement. I had written a training manual that taught the veterans the skills needed to properly care for the parrots and their habitat, but, though I had seen the healing power of the birds in action, I was still unsure of how to create a similar plan to help the vets. The men had been working with relatively tame, contented birds. And it had been in my office with me facilitating the process. The first group of birds we rescued were not as amenable to being held or petted as Sammy and Mango had been. This would not be an easy bunch for the veterans to attach to.

I shouldn't have worried. The process was natural. The tranquility of the place alone made it a healing, peaceful environment, and the veterans enjoyed doing work that made them feel of value again. The birds needed to be fed and the aviaries needed to be kept spotless. Any veterinarian will tell you these are the two primary factors necessary to ensure the health of parrots: good nutrition and proper sanitation and hygiene. Truth be told, these two are the principal factors for human health as well.

My very first volunteer was a navy vet named Mary Ellen, who'd served in Operation Desert Storm. Making sure the birds got fed was literally the only thing that got her out of her quarters each day. Mary Ellen lived in a female veterans' rehab program on the VA campus. She suffered from agoraphobia. She'd stand in the doorway of her room, willing herself to cross the threshold.

If I don't go out, she thought, if I don't take that step, who is going to take care of the birds?

She took a deep breath, she looked down at the ground, and she made herself walk. Every muscle was tense, her heart pounded, but she did it.

At first, she went through the same struggle each day, but gradually it became easier.

One day she said to me, "Having to feed the birds saved my life. I knew I had to do it so I forced myself to. Then one day I wasn't afraid to leave my room anymore."

There is a well-established theory in the treatment of phobias, obsessive-compulsive disorder, and PTSD. It is called Exposure and Response Prevention. What Mary Ellen was doing was something she was afraid to do—leave her room—and by confronting this fear and forcing herself to go out, she learned over time that nothing bad was going to happen to her. She lost the habit of fear. When her symptoms waned, she was able to go back home to Florida.

Another early volunteer, Jody, was a navy veteran and one of our first workers to really understand the personalities of the birds. She quickly started spending much of her time with Sherman, a striking macaw. With blue wings and a bright yellow chest, Sherman looked pretty, but he wouldn't hesitate to snap his large black beak if someone invaded his space. Sherman came to the sanctuary with his partner, Corky, a military macaw. Corky was bright green except for a touch of red on his face. They made a dazzling pair.

Jody felt she was unapproachable; maybe that's why she identified with a cranky old bird like Sherman. Jody lost her sense of trust during her service. In the navy, she had been sexually harassed multiple times. She endured propositions, threats, and unwanted touching. The navy command never stepped in to end the harassment, and Jody left what she had hoped would be a lifetime career. She learned she couldn't trust the very people who were supposed to keep our country safe.

Jody came home, married, and had a daughter. She became addicted to drugs and lost her daughter in a divorce. What she learned from the birds, and Sherman in particular, was how to parent. She had to be patient, or Sherman would snap. She had to be present each day and satisfy Sherman's needs, or he wouldn't trust her. She had to be firm enough that Sherman wouldn't take advantage of her, while still showing him kindness. She had to co-create the boundaries of their relationship, or Sherman would run from her. Most parents learn these lessons by bringing up their children, but Jody had been too distracted by drugs to learn these with her own daughter.

Jody earned Sherman's trust. He'd let her spend time in his aviary, something that was always hazardous for other veterans. He let her pet him sometimes, though a bit grudgingly, since, after all, he was still a cranky old bird. She learned to trust herself, too, and she came to realize she was capable of being a good parent. It was a proud day for both of us when Jody called me to say she had begun to have visits with her daughter and was working to get joint custody. Staying clean and sober was part of that, but so was what she'd learned at the sanctuary.

Another parrot, a Goffin's cockatoo named Bobbi, came to us after a drug raid. The police found her in a dresser drawer. She had plucked out all of the feathers on her chest, legs, and most of the area on her wings. All that was left was the little crest on the top of her head. She looked like nothing from this planet.

When Bobbi first came to Serenity Park, she cowered, and if you got close she postured as if she was going to bite. She stayed in the far corner of her spacious aviary. "Give her time," I told the veterans. "Let her come to you."

The veterans would stand near her, talking gently and offering little bits of apples or nuts. At first she kept her distance, but parrots are curious. She'd move close, but only to male veterans (her owner had been female). Within a few weeks, she'd come closer, watching the veterans as they worked. Finally, Bobbi let Jonathon, one of our first male veterans, tentatively pet her. Before long she was riding on his shoulder as he went about cleaning her aviary. Bobbi continued to get stronger, even though her feathers will never grow back (she bit them so deeply that the follicles were destroyed). Her sweet and curious personality shines so brightly that she is now one of the most beloved birds at the sanctuary, even with her strange appearance. She's kind and gentle enough that we can show her to our child visitors. (Her resemblance to a baby dinosaur is also a convenient lesson on how birds evolved!)

Jonathon was hoping to take her with him when he had to transfer to another VA hospital. "She means a lot to me," he said, "and I know I could make her happy."

I trusted Jonathon, and I knew he would try his best to

care for Bobbi forever. But I'd also seen firsthand how our lives can change.

"Once the birds are here," I told Jonathon gently, "they're home. No more revolving doors."

Jonathon understood. He made one final visit before he left. Bobbi hopped onto his shoulder. "It's been good," he said to her. She buried her head under his chin and cuddled against him. That wasn't the last time I saw our birds make a tough vet cry.

* * *

Not long after the sanctuary opened, I received a call from Olivia, a young punk-rock musician.

"I'm desperate," she said. "If I don't give my bird away, my landlord is going to evict me. I don't have money to get another place. I've got no other options."

Olivia told me the details. She had wanted a new pet. Her building did not allow dogs, but the unsuspecting landlord agreed to a parrot. She found an African grey parrot in a classified ad. He was baby, still needing to be weaned. Perfect, she thought. We can bond. While many people, like Olivia, are familiar with imprinting, they wrongly assume that they won't be able to form a close bond with an adult bird. They buy from breeders even while thousands of adult parrots are in need of homes. She brought the parrot home, but the breeder didn't give her clear instructions, and while she was hand-feeding him, she forced the syringe down his windpipe by accident. The bird died from breathing in the food. The breeder sold her another African grey baby at a discount, this time already weaned.

Olivia named her bird Sid Vicious. African greys are known for their intelligence, wide vocabulary, and ability to use human language. Sid was singing along with her before long. But the apartment was loud, Olivia kept late hours, and he was a wild animal. He bit her when she tried to put him in his cage for the night, he terrorized her cats, and he attacked any men she brought into her apartment.

Olivia locked him away in his cage for longer and longer periods of time. She didn't want to do this, but she also didn't want to be bitten. She was afraid for her cats, who cowered and ran away when they saw Sid. He'd chase them through her apartment and then come back with tufts of fur in his beak.

I know this story well. "Not long after you started locking him in the cage, he started screaming, am I right?"

"Yes," she said.

"Then the neighbors complained and the landlord gave you an ultimatum."

"Obviously you get a lot of calls like this," she said. "But can you still take him?"

I told Olivia we had room for Sid, but we were filling up fast. Sid would not have the luxury of having his own aviary; he would have to have a roommate. The only other African greys we had at the time were a bonded pair, and they were not likely to put up with a lone male. But there was Dandy, a female yellow-naped Amazon parrot who got along with everyone. She was alone right now because the other Amazons she lived with, Clyde and Ginger, had formed a pair.

I was worried about how Sid was going to adapt. He had been hand-raised, was accustomed to living indoors, and had never lived with another bird. He bullied and intimidated the animals he did live with. I asked Olivia to try working with a bird behaviorist first, to see if there was any way to keep him in his home. She did that, but she'd been bitten so many times she was afraid to follow up on the training regimen. "I'm done," she said, so we accepted Sid at the sanctuary.

We put him in the large security area next to Dandy. It was six by twelve feet, small by our standards but three times the size of his cage at home. If Sid and Dandy didn't get along, we would have to build a new aviary. Our policy is that all our birds should have enough room to fly.

Dandy made the first move. She was curious and friendly. She went over to where Sid was standing on the other side of the security door and said, "Mxyilovput." Or something like that. She liked to talk, but she was incomprehensible. She didn't seem to mind the speaker we had attached to the outside of the aviary so Sid could listen to the Ramones and Green Day. He sang along to the familiar music. Eventually, I thought, we would acclimate him to something softer.

Sid puffed himself up, fanned out his tail, and made a noise almost like a growl. Dandy acted like she didn't understand what he meant by those moves. When he saw that his intimidating display didn't work, he stopped being aggressive. He stared at her as if sizing her up.

They started making soft sounds at each other; they both had their own space, so they were safe. He couldn't get his beak through the cage wire if he tried, but he didn't try. Sid talked his head off and Dandy listened, occasionally interjecting something that sounded like the name of Superman's nemesis from the old comic books—unpronounceable.

Then one day I noticed cherries in Dandy's aviary.

Dandy didn't like cherries, so we rarely fed them to her. These cherries were on the ground and squished between the wires of the cages. Sid's beak was stained a deep crimson.

Had Sid been trying to feed Dandy? "Don't jump to conclusions," I told the veterans, who were rooting for Sid and Dandy to get together. "We still have to be very careful with introductions. He has a history of violence. Don't forget that fur-filled beak."

We all agreed to short, supervised visits. We would loudly clap our hands to stop aggression and keep a net or heavy bath towels handy for real emergencies.

We didn't need to worry. Dandy won Sid over almost immediately. She groomed him and fussed over him, and he fed her by holding the food delicately in his beak. He taught her new words, and she promptly garbled them. They were two distinct species from two different continents. It would be wonderful if we could all get along like that.

* * *

The people who called to give us their birds thinking their parrot would make a valuable contribution to veterans didn't understand why we couldn't automatically accept any bird offered. They didn't seem to realize that we would have to build enclosures, provide food and veterinary care, and pay the veterans who work here. Some people offered to help offset the expenses by providing monthly support. Despite the offers, the money rarely materialized once we took the birds.

One woman was downsizing and no longer had room for her cockatoo, but she wanted to be sure the place she was sending him could take adequate care of him. She'd pay us two thousand dollars a year for his expenses, she said. She visited once, saw our clean aviaries, our devoted staff, and all of the attention the birds received. The bird came. We marveled at how sweet he was and how much he loved to snuggle up to just about anyone. We took a picture of him on the shoulder of a veteran. He was kissing the bird's little beak. We sent the photo to his former family member.

The next morning, the phone rang. "What are you doing to that bird?" she demanded.

"We're loving him up. Didn't you like the picture?"

"I never knew you could touch him like that," she said.

Her bird had never been touched. He had never been let out of his cage. She'd had him for almost twenty years. I don't know how her bird managed to be as happy and loving as he was after that isolation. He must have been very resilient to still welcome human contact.

We're still waiting for the two thousand dollars.

NINE

The Parrot Whisperer

Could a greater miracle take place than for us to look through each other's eyes for an instant?

—HENRY DAVID THOREAU, *Walden*

When Lilly Love, one of our first veterans, walked into Serenity Park, she was simply curious to meet the birds. She didn't realize they would save her life. I had seen veterans healing with the help of the birds, but Lilly showed just how dramatic that healing could be. Once Serenity Park worked its magic on her, she never wanted to leave.

Lilly had been a search-and-rescue swimmer with the Coast Guard. She'd worked in the rough seas near Kodiak, Alaska, where the water is just a few degrees above freezing and the waves can be deadly. To survive this grueling job, she had gone through months of strength and stamina training. She donned a thick waterproof suit, covering her hands and even her head, to survive in the frigid water. Even with that protection, every time her helicopter lowered her into the sea, she knew she might not be coming back.

She spent five years in the service. Fishermen were swept overboard and boats sank. Lilly rescued many civilians, but she also saw people die. During her service, she was struck on the head by a boat and injured, but she fought past the pain in her body and was back on patrol as soon as her doctors allowed it.

During their patrol one day, she and her crew discovered a small boat that had lost its engine. A woman, nearly unconscious, lay in the bottom. At her side was a child's life preserver.

Lilly got into the boat. "Where's the child? Where's the child?" she asked, slapping the woman to keep her awake. Lilly knew that a person could have, at the most, an hour in the water before he or she died. At those low temperatures, their blood vessels would constrict and their extremities would grow colder. Everything but a person's heart and brain would shut down. Without that life preserver, a child would be unable to keep him or herself afloat.

"My son is dead," the woman said.

Her voice was a monotone. Lilly says she'll never forget the look on the mother's face. It wasn't just grief. It was defeat. The mother had seen her worst fears realized and given up. Lilly felt as if she were talking to someone who was already dead.

The woman's speech was slurred, and even though Lilly shook her to keep her awake, she kept closing her eyes. Her pulse was slow. Lilly had seen hypothermia before, and she knew the woman was disoriented and confused. Still, she had to find out what had happened. The boy might still be out there, cold and alone but alive.

Slowly, a word or two at a time, Lilly got the woman to speak. The engine had given out on their little boat, and they didn't have food or water. They'd waited for another boat to pass, but no one came by. Eventually, they tried to swim to shore, but less than halfway there, they realized they couldn't make it and turned back. The mother made it back to the boat. The boy didn't.

They searched the water for hours, until the wetsuit couldn't maintain Lilly's body temperature and she had to quit. She asked the helicopter to bring her back the next day, then the day after that. Any rational person would say it was too late, but Lilly kept swimming. She never found the boy's body.

The empty life jacket is the story she always goes back to in her mind, but in those dangerous waters, it wasn't the only story of loss.

Lilly was also struggling with her gender. She had been born biologically male, but she'd always known she was a woman. To the outside world, she was a tough search-and-rescue swimmer. Inside, she was a tough woman. The pain of hiding her true self, and the struggle she felt about how much she could reveal to the world, added to her torments.

Lilly drank some, to deal with the hurt she felt inside, but mostly she ignored her pain. She felt she had things under control.

The men and women of the Coast Guard didn't discuss their feelings, but Lilly knew they understood the grief and fear that came with the job. They swam in the same waters.

They saw the same deaths. When she dived into rough, nearly freezing water, Lilly trusted them to have her back.

The day after she finally left the Coast Guard, after three years with the same crew, a helicopter with her team aboard crashed. Six of the men she'd worked with died.

When she heard the news, her body crumbled. I should have been with them, Lilly thought. Why should one day make a difference? Why should I be alive?

Lilly's regret about those she failed to save and her grief over her lost comrades were her greatest psychic wounds. William Nash, a psychiatrist and former captain in the US Navy Medical Corps, has been studying the effects of guilt and loss rather than fear as the primary factors in the development of PTSD. Currently the *Diagnostic and Statistical Manual of Mental Disorders*—the "bible" of the mental health profession—lists fear as the requisite factor for developing PTSD, but the guilt from surviving a comrade in combat and killing civilians appears to be one of the most lasting sources of suffering for any veteran. Lilly watched civilians die, and she outlived most of her team.

Lilly didn't hit bottom right away. Victims of PTSD rarely do. Instead, she spent the next fifteen years spiraling downward.

She retreated to an isolated cabin located on a river near the Pacific Coast town of Yelapa, Mexico. The only way to reach it was by water. She just wanted to be warm after her time in Alaska, she joked, but it was more than that. She was retreating from people and the world. She fished and traveled the waters, so serene after the rough waves of Alaska. She spent hours just staring at the horizon. She went days without speaking. She didn't hurt herself in Mexico, but she didn't heal either. She existed. The tapes of what she'd seen still played in her head, and they grew worse with time.

When Lilly came home to the United States, she made her way to Los Angeles. The drinking that had begun in the service got worse. She'd been fairly clean in Mexico, but now she started drinking to the point where she'd pass out.

Her friends thought she was just crazy, she said. Just someone who loved living out of control. They didn't understand the depth of damage wrought by the things she'd seen. By 2001, though, they realized her behavior was dangerous. Afraid that she was going to kill herself, her friends dropped her off at the West Los Angeles VA Medical Center. The doctors diagnosed her with PTSD.

She didn't kill herself, but the most that can be said of her recovery is that she had some relatively good periods. Much of the time, though, life was tough for Lilly. Much of the time she didn't see the point of living.

She started combining alcohol with the psychotropic drugs she needed for depression, but drinking diminished the drugs' effect. She just wanted oblivion.

Lilly's struggle was harder because she had finally begun transitioning from living as a man to living as a woman. She noticed stares and whispers. She watched smiles fade as strangers realized she was a trans woman. People would spit out hateful words, and she knew physical violence was always only a step away. Worse, she realized that many people she knew, even in her Coast Guard family, would never accept her real identity. At best, they'd take pity on someone they saw as misguided; at worst, they'd hate her for being a freak. It's not always easy living as your authentic self, and the psychological pain of transitioning added to the agony she was already in. She was ready to break.

For the next five years, she would go in and out of 2 South, the psych ward within Building 500, the main medical facility at the VA. Often she was on lockdown. She could tell you which rooms were best there and which to avoid. Once, she was placed with the patients who were unresponsive; many couldn't feed themselves. Caregivers observed them through a two-way mirror. She fed one of the other patients with a spoon, then knocked on the two-way mirror. "Hey," she said, "you put me in the wrong room." They moved her, but she still didn't have her freedom. Although she could recover enough after each visit not to be a danger to herself, she never really healed. She knew she'd be visiting Building 500 again soon enough.

She'd spent so much time there that the other patients became her friends. It was like jail, she said. If you learned to get along, you could survive well enough. She had not begun to deal with the scars from her PTSD and she had not found a way to live contentedly as a trans woman.

One night, she crashed her boat into the seawall. She may have been purposefully trying to kill herself. She may just have been piloting with too many drugs in her system. Either way, it was a cry for help.

Lilly came back to the VA once again. This time, she started working in the Vet's Garden as part of her therapy. The drugs and counseling had been a bandage. Finally, nature was giving her a hint of healing. Ida Cousino touched many veterans with her important work, and Lilly was one of them. She'd always felt most comfortable outdoors. She was used to rough work, tiring her body and calming her mind. There was joy in planting something, weeding and watering to provide for another life, and the reward of watching things grow under her care.

She had always loved animals, and in Alaska she had grown to appreciate them more. She'd laughed at porpoises playfully racing beside boats. She'd seen sea lions, so awkward on land, gliding gracefully through the water. She'd watched in awe—never too close, of course—as massive grizzlies lumbered across the land. When she heard the birds at Serenity Park, she couldn't stay away.

She introduced herself. "Hi," she said, "I'm Lilly Love. Do you mind if I look at your birds?"

I didn't mind. Serenity Park can be a healing place even for those not enrolled in our program. Veterans in dire straits, like Lilly, were precisely the reason I had started the sanctuary.

At Serenity Park, Lilly finally found some solace, and her journey to healing began.

Lilly says the first thing the parrots did was bite her. Like middle schoolers, parrots will test you when you are the new kid on the block. If you aren't careful when you enter the aviaries to hang their food bowls and change their water, you could get bitten.

I introduced Lilly to Sammy. Sammy was a gentle cuddler with me. With Lilly, not so much. Lilly put it succinctly: "Sammy is a bitch."

I'd have to introduce her to another bird. Serenity Park had fewer birds in 2006 than it has now. Phoenix was a blue-and-gold macaw—or she would have been if she hadn't plucked out most of her feathers. Only a couple of sections on her back and wings hinted at the golden chest and brilliant blue body she would have had if she were healthy. Phoenix had spent most of her life inhaling air thick with her owner's cigarette smoke. Flying is strenuous, so birds have evolved to have a higher volume of oxygen in their bloodstreams than mammals; because she was breathing in so much smoke, Phoenix had developed a chronic cough. When we picked her up, her cage was filled with droppings and feathers. She had no enrichment activities, no games of any kind. All she had was a bowl with a couple of sunflower seeds and some Fritos, because, her owner claimed, "that's what she likes to eat." Though she'd lived with the same man for eighteen years, he didn't even bother to get off his couch when we came to pick her up. He didn't want to miss the end of the golf tournament on television.

Phoenix was a fear biter, unlike Sammy, who bit because she just didn't like Lilly. Phoenix had learned not to trust people, and she certainly didn't trust Lilly. I suspected, though, that she just needed a gentle hand. Years of anxiety and boredom had shown her that the world was an untrustworthy place; we had to demonstrate a different reality to her. I explained to Lilly how to get to know the birds. No sudden moves, I told her, and give the parrot time to get used to you. Positioning herself on a chair near Phoenix's cage, Lilly made frequent eye contact; unlike many predatory animals, parrots do not see eye contact as threatening. Lilly was fascinated by Phoenix, even if she wasn't the loveliest bird in the world, with her bumpy, naked skin. Perhaps that physical manifestation of mental anguish drew Lilly in. She saw a creature in pain, and pain was something she understood. She was willing to sit there and wait.

When Phoenix got to know her a little better, she let Lilly

come closer to her in the aviary. Within a few weeks, she cautiously approached Lilly. She turned her head to get a better look. Lilly spoke gently. Phoenix hopped one step, then another, until she was by Lilly's side. It might take an hour for her to get in close, but the barriers were gradually coming down. Soon, the two would sit together for an hour or more.

Eventually, Lilly was able to hold Phoenix and gently groom what few feathers she had left. Sometimes the two would just look at each other. As they got closer, the trust felt palpable. Watching them, I know they were completely comfortable together. Lilly started to smile more. Her shoulders relaxed. Phoenix began to hop more quickly to Lilly's side when she came in, and she even bounced up and down in a little greeting. I couldn't hear what Lilly was saying to Phoenix, but I could hear a gentle laugh here and there.

One day, Lilly came to me, worried about Phoenix. She hadn't eaten since the day before. She didn't bob up and down in greeting or even leave her perch. I noticed that her abdomen was distended.

"Let's get her to the veterinarian," I said.

"Is she going to be okay?" asked Lilly.

"I think so, but she needs help," I said.

I suspected that Phoenix was egg-bound. An egg-bound bird has an egg trapped somewhere in her reproductive system. The problem can be fatal. Although there are many reasons a bird might suffer from this problem, it's most common in birds who are malnourished and whose movements have been restricted. A bird who dined on Fritos and lived in a small cage, like Phoenix, would be predisposed to the problem, and it might have been one of the reasons her owner gave her up. Phoenix had plenty of room to move and a nutritious diet at the sanctuary, but her body might still be suffering from years of neglect.

Lilly cradled Phoenix on the way to the veterinarian. She whispered gently and stroked Phoenix's feathers, but Lilly's body was rigid with worry. Once the veterinarian was able to free the egg, Lilly relaxed and smiled. She stroked Phoenix and told her how brave she was. I explained to Lilly that this might happen again, and that the problem could be fatal. Lilly nodded. "Right now, though, we saved her. She has this day."

Nurturing Phoenix, and allowing Phoenix to love her in return, helped Lilly come to terms with her identity as a woman. Men can, of course, be nurturers as well, but our culture tends to view caregiving as a female task. Taking on that role with Phoenix let Lilly explore her feelings as a woman, and in a way that was far less threatening than caring for a human. The parrots, Lilly says, became her children.

Phoenix continued to become egg-bound. The last time, the veterinarian wasn't able to save her. "I'm so sorry," Lilly whispered when she was gone.

We all grieved for Phoenix, but Lilly most of all. She sat quietly and stared at the empty cage. "Goodbye, Phoenix," she said at last. "Thank you."

But though she cried, she didn't fall apart, and her progress didn't stop. Lilly had seen many deaths in the Coast Guard. She'd buried them in the back of her brain and carried on, and that pain almost killed her. When Phoenix died, she let herself grieve. We had a funeral and buried Phoenix's ashes, and Lilly read a poem. She planted beautiful flowers on her grave. By saying goodbye, Lilly could move on. She still misses Phoenix, but that loss didn't overwhelm her.

Lilly tells me that, for her, the healing began as soon as she entered our grounds. Even though the birds wanted no part of her those first days, their presence comforted her. In the quiet peace of the sanctuary, her mind was temporarily quiet as well. As she bonded with Phoenix, the feeling grew stronger. She saw this damaged bird's pain clearly on its damaged body. Phoenix was wounded, just as Lilly was, and the two of them learned to trust another being as they grew close. She had spent years suffering from the guilt over those she could not save, about being the one still alive while others died, and now she had someone she could help in a tangible way.

Lilly's healing was typical of what we see in most veterans at Serenity Park, though it progressed more quickly than usual. Over a few weeks, she made connections with the birds. The barriers she'd built between herself and the world slowly dissolved. She began living in the moment, not in the past that had wounded her. When you're with the parrots, she says, "you have to stop playing those tapes in your head. You must be fully present. If you're not, you might lose a finger." She liked to recite an oft-quoted saying: "The present is a gift. That's why they call it the present."

As she grew closer to the birds, she began opening up to people. If the parrots have become family for Lilly, so have the other veterans.

"We're all screwed up," she says, "but we're all screwed up in the same boat. The men and women at Serenity Park understand each other. Look at David," she says, pointing. "When he got here he could barely speak and wouldn't look you in the eye. Now he's friends with all the vets here." David came to Serenity Park at the recommendation of his social worker after seven surgeries to resolve a traumatic brain injury from an improvised explosive device. The surgeries helped with the brain bleeds and swelling but not his cognitive functioning, so David had significant memory loss, poor impulse control, and little outward emotional expression, making it difficult for him to communicate. One of our true success stories, David learned so many job skills and so many social skills while volunteering at Serenity Park that he was able to get employment as a chef "on the outside," a main goal of our program.

One day Lilly came to me to announce that her psychiatrist had taken her off her antidepressants, and she'd never felt better. Those medications are not meant to be taken for life. The aim is to give the patient a boost in her treatment and make her feel as if the light at the end of the tunnel is not an oncoming train. Depression sucks the color from the world and makes the present struggle feel endless, and the drugs help a patient escape that overwhelming darkness and hopelessness. But as a person's brain chemistry stabilizes, more sustaining improvements should come from psychological treatment methods such as cognitive behavioral therapy. CBT helps a person change what are known as ANTs—automatic negative thoughts, those tapes we too often allow "free rent in our heads," as the AA program astutely says. For Lilly, those tapes stopped playing, or at least didn't play as often, and she was able to begin feeling the other multilayered benefits of her CBT.

Lilly agrees that Serenity Park works even for those who are not part of the program. Once a week, dozens of veterans come by to visit the food bank we operate. Before picking up their groceries, most take a few moments to visit the birds.

"If you look at them, you can see the healing," says Lilly.

These days, Lilly is our parrot wrangler. She works each day trying to socialize the birds. You could say she's also a parrot whisperer, but with parrots there's not much whispering. She is more of a parrot sweet-talker.

Lilly tries to interact with each bird daily. Some of the birds come running to her. They let her hold and pet them. Sometimes, she says, the birds just make her want to hug them. She lets the birds come to her, but only if they are willing. That is an essential credo of Serenity Park: the parrots interact with you only if they want to. The birds need to have that choice, that sense of autonomy. If a bird isn't interested in her, Lilly is content to just look. Like us, the birds have their moods, and Lilly gets that.

Making eye contact is no small thing for Lilly. She describes how she believes she can see a soul looking back at her. In that moment, she feels a profound connection to the birds. While there is something almost metaphysical in the way Lilly explains it, that connection is something that helps keep her firmly rooted in the world.

Lilly is no longer suicidal. Her friends aren't worried that she'll have an accident on her boat. She's given up alcohol. She has a boyfriend. She lives on her boat not to escape the world or to do penance in some way for her Coast Guard comrades. She lives on the boat because she loves the water. "I'm blessed and grateful," she says.

TEN

Finding Forgiveness

Yet, love, mere love, is beautiful indeed.

—Elizabeth Barrett Browning

When Matt Simmons, the yeoman who'd served in Iraq, showed up at Serenity Park, we were still rather small, with only a few aviaries.

I was hosing down the parrot enclosures. I wore a business suit covered in overalls and rubber boots. My two volunteer veterans had medical appointments that day, and the parrots had to be cared for. I was not going to skimp on sanitation, even if it meant I'd show up at an important meeting a little wet and dirty.

I hoped the man in the New Directions uniform heading down the path to the sanctuary was coming to help me.

"You here to volunteer?" I called out.

Matt wasn't sure what he would find when he walked into Serenity Park. His family had had a dog growing up, but he knew nothing whatsoever about birds. Still, hard work was always something he could do.

He barely smiled but let me know he was available for whatever I needed.

I took him into an enclosure. It's rarely a good idea for people who don't know the parrots to enter their space, but I knew the two birds in this enclosure wouldn't hurt anyone, even a complete stranger like Matt. They were babies, and wounded ones at that. These two birds were part of a local flock of wild parrots. Some kind of animal had attacked them, and they'd been thrown out of their nests. They were small, abandoned, and injured.

I had purchased soft foam, the kind people use to line music room walls, to act as a cushion in case the baby parrots fell. It was stretched across the entire aviary. I picked up one of the baby birds, a lilac-crowned Amazon (like the one my friend Robin bought years before), and wrapped her in a towel. She was old enough to have grown her lovely green feathers, set off by a red forehead and lilac head, though some had been torn in the attack. She would grow to be a medium-sized parrot, but she was still small enough to be in the nest; you could hold her in one hand. She squawked, but weakly for a parrot. "She needs medicine, and she needs to have her wounds cleaned," I explained.

While we worked, I talked quietly to her, trying to calm her. She'd relax a little, at least until we touched a sore spot. "It's okay, Ruby; you're doing great. You're such a brave, good girl," I said softly. Ruby objected, but not strongly.

Afterward, we pulled out the old foam and put new foam down. It was heavy and bulky, even for a large man like Matt.

I have no idea how I would have managed if he hadn't been there.

"Why do we need this, anyway?" Matt asked.

"I don't want her to get hurt more if she falls," I explained. "But moving it to clean it isn't that easy," I admitted.

"A net would make a lot more sense," he said. He had been at Serenity Park for less than an hour, and he was already trying to improve the way we did things.

Matt told me he wasn't sure at first that the program could help him at all. He didn't understand parrots. He didn't understand how dragging dirty foam and cleaning cuts on a bird could help his PTSD. He didn't understand how this woman in a business suit and galoshes could help anyone. He was willing to try, though, and that's the biggest step we can take.

I taught Matt how to take care of Ruby, as well as her sister Maggie, on his own. Parrots, even sick ones, have strong beaks, and in those first few days, they both used theirs on Matt when they got the chance. They didn't get many chances, though. Matt learned quickly exactly how to hold them in a towel, and he cleaned their wounds and gave them their medicine efficiently. He had big, strong hands, but with those little creatures he was gentle.

Healing often hurts. As far as Ruby and Maggie could tell, Matt was just making that pain worse.

Over time the birds got stronger, and their wounds closed. Their natural curiosity emerged, and they started climbing around the aviary. They grew larger. Their missing feathers filled in. Soon they learned to fly. Physically, they were doing well, but they were still young, the equivalent of human toddlers, and they had no parents.

Matt kept coming back. He had grown to care what happened to the little birds and enjoyed watching them progress. Ruby and Maggie watched Matt as well, a little wary of this huge creature who had hurt them. They'd squawk when he entered, giving him plenty of leeway, but they didn't attack.

In the next cage over, a mature double yellow-headed Amazon named Joey lived by himself. Like Ruby and Maggie, he was green, but he had a bright yellow head and forehead and hints of red on his wings. He was a few inches longer and a few ounces heavier than Ruby and Maggie would ever be, and when they were young he towered over them. Joey was between twenty and thirty years old. He'd had a loving companion, but when that man died at a young age from AIDS, his family and friends had to take care of his bird. Instead of adopting him themselves, they gave Joey to a pet store (the fate of many long-lived birds whose owners die before they do). Joey didn't have a mate or a flock. He was cranky, maybe from grief, maybe from fear, or maybe he just didn't like humans, and he'd bite people at the store who tried to pet him. When the store realized they couldn't make money off him, they allowed a rescuer to bring him to us. Because he'd been aggressive at the store, we initially kept Joey away from the other birds. Matt noticed that Joey was watching the two younger birds. Joey would talk to Ruby and Maggie. He wasn't squawking or threatening; he seemed almost kind, Matt thought.

"I think he wants to be with them," said Matt.

I wasn't sure. "Parrots are always curious, but that doesn't mean he likes them. They're a different species. And he's a male. They aren't big enough to defend themselves."

"Let's watch them. I think it might work. I'll be here the whole time," said Matt.

I realized that Matt had started spending more time with Ruby and Maggie than I did. He watched them at length every day. I decided to give it a chance, at least for a few afternoons. We put Joey in with the two younger birds. Matt sat in the aviary, guarding the little ones. Joey didn't attack. He groomed them. He sat by them on the perch. We decided to leave them together for a trial run.

"Lorin," Matt said one afternoon, "can you come over here?"

He led me to Ruby's enclosure. "What are they doing?" asked Matt. Joey was bobbing his head slightly, and Ruby had her beak deep inside his. "Is she biting his tongue?"

She was eating. Parrots feed their young by eating food, breaking it down, and regurgitating it back to their children in an easily digestible form. Joey was regurgitating, just like any good parrot mother or father would do in the wild. But Joey was not kin, not even the same species. This was a remarkable act of altruism, something social scientists tend to attribute mainly to humans. Joey had taken it upon himself to care for the babies.

"They're a family," Matt said quietly.

Matt worked hard at the sanctuary, cleaning aviaries, chopping vegetables and fruit for forage trays, repairing perches. But he'd always make time to be with Ruby, Maggie, and now Joey. He spent weeks just watching them quietly, letting them know that he wasn't a danger. They kept their distance, but they didn't threaten him.

One day Ruby flew to his shoulder. "I can't believe it," he whispered. "I think she likes me."

She crawled down to his hands and let him pet her under the wings. Joey was part of Ruby's new flock, but she was telling Matt that he was a part as well.

"Good girl, good girl," he said quietly.

It felt like forgiveness, he told me later. This little wild creature was choosing to spend time with the big, scary human who had held her tightly in a towel. She had suffered at his hands while he medicated her, but that was over. She was ready to give him another chance.

I noticed tears on Matt's face, and I turned away to give him time alone.

Ruby had been wounded, but she'd found healing at Serenity Park. Her heart was open, and it was time for Matt to open his, too.

* * *

When Ruby flew to him, Matt felt that she must have seen some good in him. And that gave Matt permission to feel something good about himself. Maybe he was worth caring for. Maybe he wasn't too far gone.

Matt had seen things that wounded his soul, and he had wounded others, but here at the sanctuary he was able to heal another creature. He learned that caring for others is often a way of caring for yourself. Matt had a gentle heart but he'd been too guarded to let himself nurture others, especially after developing PTSD. Matt was learning to break down his barriers and surrender.

I was spending all my time at the sanctuary, and Matt started opening up to me in a way he'd never opened up to anyone. It was as if breaking down one barrier made it easier for the others to fall.

I was Matt's boss at Serenity Park, so he wasn't my patient. "Talk to your therapist and your sponsor and keep working your program," I said. I was hoping he would maintain this trajectory of growth. But Matt liked talking to me. He didn't hide any of his past, even though some of it shamed him. It was easier to talk to me than to his therapist, he said, but I insisted he continue to be in treatment.

"It's not the same. Your therapist will be able to help you in ways I can't," I told him. Maybe, though, I could help him in other ways. He needed to open up to people in his daily life, not just in a clinical setting. He was sharing in group therapy, with the men at mealtimes, with anyone who would sit still for a few minutes.

I talk to all the veterans at Serenity Park, and I care about their therapeutic progress. I'm not their therapist, though. The birds and the work are the therapy. But with Matt, it felt more like talking to a colleague than an employee. I found myself sharing with him as well. It felt good to be wanted not just as a therapist or boss but as a friend.

Matt's healing was more dramatic than I had seen with most of the other veterans; his progress reminded me of Lilly's. He believed the parrots gave him his life back, and he was forever in their debt. Once he'd experienced that moment of forgiveness with Ruby, he was completely devoted to healing the parrots and to healing himself.

Most of the veterans coming through Serenity Park don't have the kind of epiphany Matt did. For them, healing is a slower process. They come to us refusing to make eye contact, staying away from people, shut deeply within themselves. It's only after many weeks that we see them open up. And I'm sorry to say that some of the problem lies with modern psychological and psychiatric treatment itself. Sometimes practitioners do more harm than good.

Drugs are often the first method of treatment for people suffering from psychological disorders. Psychotropic drugs change the chemistry of the brain, and they can have significant side effects. For many disorders, such as mild depression, drugs may be no more effective than placebos. The benefits may not be real, but the side effects are. People gain weight, lose their sex drive, and even have long-term health problems. Some ethnic groups are more susceptible to these negative effects; Asians, for example, can experience adverse side effects at lower doses than other ethnicities do. Writing a prescription is easier than urging patients to make changes in their lifestyle and outlook, but it can be far more harmful, both in the short and long term. And patients often hope for quick fixes, miracle cures, and may not want to put in the required effort to make behavioral changes.

For people with substance abuse problems, relying on drugs for solutions can be even more problematic. These are men and women who have tried to self-medicate through drugs and alcohol. Having them take drugs as a cure-all is, at best, teaching them that the same old solutions work, though the drugs come from a pharmacy rather than a dealer. At worst, we're setting them on a downward spiral; they begin taking the legally prescribed drugs and end up abusing whatever they can get their hands on.

Of course, there are those with serious psychiatric conditions who do require long-term treatment with medications. But many veterans' problems are more than manageable with nontraditional methods. Our society has come to rely upon therapists as people who solve our problems. Instead, we need to teach people to solve their own problems. Our approach to mental health should be far broader than therapy and drugs alone. It should start in the school system, where children could learn things like managing negative peer pressure, resolving conflicts, healthy communication, setting appropriate boundaries, dealing with life transitions, and basic self-care to keep them from developing psychological problems. An investment in this kind of mental health education early in life could prevent much psychological suffering later.

At Serenity Park, we set about restoring psychological balance by being in nature—our little outdoor, peaceful refuge. To that we add a sense of purpose, something every well-lived life requires. Other components of our program also contribute to successful recovery. We encourage veteran camaraderie to foster a sense of belonging which helps build self-worth. Combined with support for healthy conflict resolution and substance use reduction, our approach helps veterans find a better way to live their lives. If that were all there was to it, though, then many other VA programs would produce the same effects as Serenity Park.

But here we add the parrots. The bonds the vets make with the parrots have their own restorative effects. What we consider success is when veterans learn a new way of interacting with the world, of focusing on others. They learn the profound power of empathy and compassion, crucial factors in psychological well-being and in rebuilding relationships. They learn to be outside of their own heads and firmly in the present (if they don't, they might feel the power of a parrot's beak).

When I visited Japan, I researched Morita therapy for the

treatment of nervosity. The intention of this therapy is to get people out of their negative thoughts and to become more outward, to direct their thoughts more toward the community and the world. An important emphasis of Morita therapy is on action rather than self-analysis, and the "cure" is losing oneself in productive work, giving oneself over to something bigger than just oneself.

The veterans spent time in group and individual therapy, but where was a meaningful purpose for them outside of their recovery? Many veterans had joined the military because they valued the idea of being of service, and, with their battles done, they had lost their purpose. The parrots helped them find a way to serve again. Purposeful work provides a wellspring for veteran recovery.

The benefits the veterans get from Serenity Park translate into long-term sobriety, community involvement, permanent employment, stable housing, and reunification with friends and family—what it takes to be successful in society.

* * *

Matt woke up before dawn to do his job at New Directions. He worked in the kitchen preparing breakfast for all the veterans living there. Then he came to Serenity Park and worked until dark. The parrots helped him to keep going no matter what.

Within weeks, I knew that I could leave him alone with all the birds, not just Ruby (though he spent time with his little flock every day). He knew many of them as well as I did. He knew who was likely to pick locks and try to escape (we've never had a successful escapee, but it pays to be vigilant). He knew who would attack if he turned his back. He knew which ones would scream until they got attention. Matt had never allowed himself to connect to anything the way he connected to the birds. He'd worked hard in the military, and he'd worked hard at building his computer company. This was different. This was passion.

I respected him, and I knew I could trust him. It wasn't that I disregarded the terrible things he'd done in his life. It was that I could tell that something fundamental had changed. I could see real love between him and the birds. When he talked to Ruby, Maggie, and Joey, he was talking to friends.

He began teaching other veterans at the sanctuary. At first he did little things. He showed them how to prepare the food and the proper way to clean a cage. He showed them how to hold a parrot without hurting him or her, and without losing a finger. He showed them which parrots could be easily trusted and which they had to watch out for. Once he was able to form bonds with animals, forming bonds with people became easier. If the veterans were struggling to stay clean, Matt would help. Giving his fellow sailors and soldiers advice about birds quickly became mentoring them on all aspects of their recovery.

Human touch can be tremendously healing, but because of the numbing and social avoidance stemming from PTSD, many men and women with the disorder rarely come in close contact with people other than family. Matt made a point of touching men on the shoulder and even hugging them if they were ready. He knew how healing Ruby's touch had been for him. He found ways to get the veterans to interact with the birds. It's easier to say "Julius needs attention" than to say "You need a hug." The birds offered the warmth and contact the veterans needed in a nonthreatening way.

He worked with the men, but he also just spent time with them. They'd sit on our benches and picnic tables together. "How's the recovery going?" Matt would ask, or "Have you been making it to your meetings?" Sometimes he'd just ask if they'd caught last night's football game. Many veterans liked having someone accompany them on doctor visits, and Matt would sit with them for hours in Building 500 while they went through medical procedures or waited for test results. He helped them fill out the paperwork for their disability benefits. He found a way to make contact, to form a connection. Anything that drew the veterans outside of themselves and back into society helped.

Matt became the veterans' alpha wolf. When people think of alpha wolves, they often think of aggressive, domineering animals who rule the pack. It's not like that, though. Alphas will risk anything to care for others in their pack. They don't rule over them; they protect them. They're father figures, not bullies. Matt was strong, and he was dominant, but he was not domineering. The men responded by coming to him for guidance.

Matt took on increasing responsibilities even though I respected that he needed time to work on his recovery as well. He ordered all of the seeds and nuts and ended up getting us a veteran's discount. He saved us a great deal of money. Within months, he took over the assignment of big brothers/sisters and little brothers/sisters, making sure the more experienced veterans working and volunteering at Serenity Park were properly matched with newcomers. He was a good role model for the other staff. We needed someone like him at Serenity Park.

"When you graduate from your program, let's talk about a full-time job here. We could use your help," I said.

Matt smiled. "I never want to leave."

ELEVEN

Being Chosen

The most common way people give up their
power is by thinking they don't have any.

—ALICE WALKER

All the newcomers to Serenity Park are expected to be clean
and sober. We suggest AA meetings and *The Big Book*. Without a strong commitment to recovery, they do not have a
firm foundation on which to rebuild their lives. A few we can't
reach. A few begin to heal but can't stay on the path to sobriety. We agonize over them. Many, fortunately, find some
healing through the birds. A few stand out.

Duke stood out. Duke grew up around biker gangs, and
when he finished his military service, he began hanging
around the bikers' world. He loves working with and riding
bikes, and he looks the part, with a burly physique and an
impressive mustache.

I met Duke during a Veteran Stand Down event on the
campus of the West Los Angeles VA. He was living in the

Domiciliary, Building 212, where the VA houses patients in need of long-term medical care. He was walking around the grounds, just taking a break. I had a million things to organize, but someone had to drive the golf cart to shuttle the veterans who couldn't walk that well and I was acting as chauffeur. I saw Duke coming toward me. He wasn't young, but he was strong and healthy-looking, and, most important, he didn't seem to have anywhere to go.

I've never been shy about asking for help when it's needed. "Hey," I shouted. "Do you think you could do a job for me?"

That's how he became part of the sanctuary, and in some ways he's never left.

Duke had spent most of his adult life behind bars. Before 2012, he'd spent fourteen of the prior twenty years locked up. He doesn't blame his problems on his time in the military service. He had taken drugs and committed crimes before he enlisted, and he'd gone back to that lifestyle when he finished his service. Getting drugs and money was all that really mattered to him. He latched onto gangs that needed someone to do their dirty work. When they wanted something done—intimidation, robbery, beating someone up—they called on Duke.

Duke didn't just hurt others and their families, he hurt the people in his own life who were close to him. He knew what he was doing was wrong. He just didn't care. He liked the money, and he liked the excitement. Most important, he liked the drugs the crimes could buy. It was a job for him, the only one he really knew. He was comfortable in that world. As Duke says, "Some guys take a briefcase to work. I brought a gun."

People tried to reach Duke. His wife told him she would

leave him if he didn't change his life. He never quit, but in spite of her threats, she never left. They first met in high school, but Duke wasn't ready to settle down, so she married another man. Duke never stopped thinking about her, and she became the one thing he cared about other than drugs. When her husband died, she started writing to Duke in prison. They married when he was released, but he'd always get locked up again. They were never able to settle into building a life together. He cared for his wife, but he didn't care enough to change his life.

Duke says he often felt guilty about committing crimes, but he didn't have much choice once he was sentenced the first time. The California prison system has a 65 percent recidivism rate. Duke swears it feels like 90 percent. Once you get a state prison identification number, you expect you'll go back. Duke figured that he'd be in prison again whether or not he kept committing crimes. The police knew his face. If trouble happened anywhere near him, he was one of the usual suspects.

He doesn't have much formal education—even though he's obviously intelligent. If you ask him if he's ever tried to live a straight life, he says: "They set me on a corner with two hundred bucks. I'd spent fifty or sixty on a motel room for a night, and then I'd be pretty much broke. What else could I do? Who'd hire me?"

Duke says he must have talked to thirty or forty prison counselors over the years. They were useless as far as he was concerned.

"I'd talk to them, and in a minute, they'd diagnose me with something. They put a label on me and had all the answers. They didn't know me at all. I have certificates in every program they offered: anger management, conflict avoidance, family planning. None of them were worth the paper they were printed on. None of those guys had a clue." The counselors, he felt, wanted to slap a diagnosis on him so they could move on to someone else.

Duke saw right through the system and its meager efforts at rehabilitation, but he played along. Following the rules kept him out of trouble. He knew many of the other inmates, and he had a tough enough exterior so no one bothered him too badly. He used the time in prison to make new connections and make plans for the crimes he'd commit on the outside. In a way, he viewed prison as a college for crime. He could get all the drugs he wanted. He relaxed with his friends. The only thing he didn't have was women. Incarceration wasn't going to deter him from living the only life he knew.

In 2012, his wife said he had to clean up or get lost. She'd made the threat in the past, but this time Duke saw that something was different. She meant it. She was tired. She wasn't getting any younger, and her patience was gone. She found three programs that would accept him.

The day he was released from prison, she drove him to the VA. He didn't want to lose her. He thought about getting older, and he could see himself dying alone. He knew the guys in the biker gang wouldn't sit by his bedside. Duke wanted someone in his life, and he wanted his wife specifically. He knew she was patient; she'd put up with him for longer than he could have hoped. I've taken her for granted, he thought. He'd never let himself feel guilt before, but he felt it now. He loved his wife. He was going to give up crime or she'd be out of his life for good.

Besides, he desperately needed medical care. Years of

drug abuse were finally taking their toll on his aging body. He'd suffered a stroke. He felt bloated and tired. His blood pressure was dangerously high. He hadn't had his teeth fixed in twenty years, and they were a sorry sight. His rehab program was close to Building 212. He needed to take care of his health or he wouldn't have much time left.

It was while he was staying at the VA, going to this rehab program and undergoing medical treatment, that he came across me in the golf cart. He spent the rest of the day driving veterans to and from the Stand Down event at the sanctuary, though Matt and I made sure he took a break to enjoy the food and the music.

I could tell Duke needed help, though he was the last guy who'd ever admit that himself. He looked tough, closed off, maybe even a little angry. He also looked lost. "Why don't you start volunteering here?" I asked him. He agreed.

Duke knew he was getting better physically, but his mind was still the same. He didn't really want to leave the drugs and alcohol behind. He had nothing against the program he was in, but it wasn't working for him. He needed to keep busy and he liked Serenity Park. He'd kept pigeons as a boy and had an affinity for anything with wings. He was willing to give the program a try.

Like all the veterans who work or volunteer for us, Duke was expected to arrive at the sanctuary at 7:30 a.m.

After he'd been with us a couple of weeks, Duke came to me. "Can I get here a little earlier?"

He'd always been on time. He'd done everything we'd asked. He was good with the birds. There was no reason he couldn't arrive a little earlier. I knew from watching the other veterans that it could only help him.

Duke started coming a little earlier, then a lot earlier. Soon, he was arriving at the Sanctuary at 5:30 a.m.

Matt came early, too. He supervised the other veterans, so he had to be there when we opened, but he also wanted to see what Duke was up to. One morning, Matt arrived at dawn. The parrots were just beginning to wake up and stretch in the soft early light. Duke was sitting in an enclosure with Stevie, sharing his breakfast. Stevie was the outgoing cockatoo who called everyone "sweetheart." If anyone entered his aviary, though, Stevie would swoop down and bite. We had warned our veterans to watch their backs around him. But there Stevie sat, comfortable on Duke's shoulder. Duke would hold out his spoon to give a little bite to Stevie, then take one himself.

"Me and Stevie are just having a little bowl of oatmeal. His favorite is cinnamon raisin."

Matt laughed. Here were a tough guy and a tough bird just sharing a cozy little breakfast together.

Matt told me about Duke and Stevie. "I've got a theory," he said. Matt said he believes the birds recognize pieces of themselves in the veterans, and they pick the men and women who are right for them. The skittish bird picks the man who needs a little extra hand-holding. The bird who is never sure how to act around others picks out the socially awkward woman. One troublemaker finds another. Duke and Stevie were both tough on the exterior, but when they trusted someone they could be gentle. I wasn't sure there was any scientific evidence for Matt's observation, but it was obvious that Stevie saw something in Duke that he didn't see in anyone else. The evidence was sitting in front of Matt, eating breakfast.

"I've been through prison riots," he told Matt. "I wasn't scared. But that first day, when Stevie flew to me and landed on my shoulder, I was terrified. Now when I get to the sanctuary, he flies to his door. I ask him if he wants me to come in, and he flies to his perch. It's like he wants to talk to me. It's like he picked me out."

That feeling of being chosen is something that comes up again and again in my talks with the veterans. These men and women have been through hell, and they usually put up a front to keep the world away. Though always, inside, there's a person who just wants to be singled out and recognized. To be told he or she is special. When the veterans get that affirmation, they start to open up in other ways. Being needed helps chisel away at their defenses.

Duke was used to making people afraid; being wanted was something new. He responded to Stevie and sought him out. Most of the time, when he got to the sanctuary early, Duke would just sit and talk to Stevie. They had long, one-way conversations, at least if you don't count the occasional interjection of "Hello, sweetheart."

"When I talked to all those counselors," Duke said to Matt, "they thought they had me all figured out. Stevie just listens. No judgment. I swear I learned more in a few months talking to him than I did in fourteen years talking to counselors. Honest to God, it's like he saw me and said, 'Now there's a guy who needs help.' And all I have to pay him is a pet and a little oatmeal."

Duke was able to tell Stevie that taking drugs had stopped being fun years ago. They'd answered a need he'd never acknowledged he had: to numb himself against his insecurities. Violence wasn't just about making money. He liked feeling tough, he liked putting up a facade to frighten people away. He was protecting himself. Inside, though, he wasn't tough at all. He was afraid. Once Duke was able to acknowledge these things to himself, he was able to start recovery.

When I arrived each morning, Duke would be talking to Stevie. If Duke noticed someone watching, the two would run through their little set of tricks. Stevie would climb down and groom Duke's mustache for him. "Better than any comb," Duke claimed. Stevie would mimic giving Duke kisses on the cheek. Duke would laugh like a father proud of his child's latest accomplishment. Watching these two tough old guys together, you'd catch a glimpse of the sweet children hidden inside.

"We understand each other," Duke said. "I've been in a cage most of my life, and he'll be in a cage the rest of his. I feel like I'm bringing him a little freedom." Though the enclosure is far larger than the typical parrot cage, it still keeps Stevie in.

For Duke, a large part of recovery was just changing the space in which he lived. I don't mean that just metaphorically. He recognized, after hours of talking, that he couldn't stay in his old neighborhood any longer. Eventually he realized that if he saw the same people, he'd end up committing the same crimes, he'd buy drugs, and he'd be back in prison. Or the police would pick him up because he looked like someone else who'd committed a crime. He vowed to spend each day with the parrots, not back on the streets.

Duke stayed clean. When his time in his rehab program ended, he volunteered at Serenity Park for a while. He wanted to be with the birds even if he wasn't in an official program. Then he and his wife moved to a new city. He got his health under control, and now, with proper medical attention and without the drugs, he feels better than he has since he was a young man.

He still thinks about Stevie every morning. "I know it's a strange thing for an old convict to say," he says, "but I miss that little bird. I miss talking to him." He's going to visit him someday, and he thinks Stevie will remember him. Of course he will. The birds always recognize old friends who visit.

Each day is a gift for Duke. He now lives his life caring for others. He can't take back his past, but he can live in the present. His wife isn't threatening to leave anymore. She's talking about the future. And so is Duke.

TWELVE

A Blessed Baby

As far as we can discern, the sole purpose of
human existence is to kindle a light of meaning in the darkness of mere being.

—CARL JUNG

People often ask me exactly how bird therapy works. How
do parrots and veterans heal one another? When I describe
the process, it sounds like a little manual labor and a lot of
downtime just hanging out together. But it's more than that.
It's part of nature therapy.

My practice had been heavily influenced by the relatively
new fields of ecopsychology and deep ecology. Developed by
Theodore Roszak, the original focus of ecopsychology was
the connection between mental health problems and the destruction of our global ecosystems. Roszak claimed there
needed to be a standard of sanity that included how we treat
and respond to our natural world. Depression, routinely
referred to in psychotherapy circles as "the common cold
of mental illness," is seen in ecopsychology to be directly

correlated with imbalances in our environmental condition. Roszak asked each of us to look not only at what we do to the earth but also at what the earth does for us.

What especially appealed to the animal lover in me was that ecopsychology was rooted in deep ecology. Arne Naess, a Norwegian philosopher, coined the term "deep ecology" to refer to Gandhian-like direct action to avert the environmental catastrophe portrayed in Rachel Carson's book *Silent Spring*. Carson showed how pesticides worked their way through the ecosystem, ultimately causing birds' eggs to become so thin that they would crack and the embryos inside would die. Birds like the bald eagle and brown pelican were threatened with extinction until some of these pesticides were better regulated. In a similar way, the destruction of the earth hurts humans; harm to one part of our environment inevitably causes injury to another. Deep ecology seeks to stop this damage. This requires humans to develop compassion beyond any falsely perceived species boundaries. Human needs and planetary needs can be seen as one; the earth's depletion by industrial society becomes our own depletion. For example, our immune systems are weakened by toxic-waste spills, which cause the contamination of our water or air; we become depressed when we hear of wildlife extinctions and anxious when we wonder what will happen to the oceans as a result of yet another oil leak.

Similarly, in *When Technology Wounds: The Human Consequences of Progress*, Chellis Glendinning writes about the psychological damage caused by the advancement of technology. Rates of cancer, a modern disease resulting from modern lifestyles, have exploded since the Industrial Revolution. So, too, have many psychological ailments. Televisions, computers, smartphones, innovations that seem to bring individuals closer, often, ironically, isolate us.

To heal, then, we need to stay in touch with nature. We need to acknowledge that we're just another of earth's creatures and connect to the planet we've evolved on. Spending time with the parrots helps to draw the veterans back into the tremendously healing power of nature itself.

The process works differently with each veteran. Matt's belief that the veterans gravitate toward birds who are similar to them grew stronger as we began to work with more men and women. We didn't set out to match veterans with parrots, but as the veterans worked in the sanctuary, they naturally gravitated toward birds with whom they felt a particular bond.

When Thomas, one of the veterans who came to us after three tours of duty in Iraq and Afghanistan during Operation Iraqi Freedom/Operation Enduring Freedom, began working at the sanctuary, he found healing in just such a bond.

Thomas was born and raised in the Texas Panhandle. His mother struggled for more than two days to give birth, and the midwife feared that Thomas wouldn't make it. Blood soaked through the bedding. His mother was too weak to push. When Thomas was finally born, she couldn't raise her arms to hold him, but she smiled when she heard his strong cries. He had not just survived the struggle, he had thrived. He must be special.

"My mother always said I was a blessed baby," Thomas said.

He was the middle child in a family with two brothers and four sisters. His mother and father are still married after forty-four years. His four sisters doted on him.

He attended college off and on. Most of the time, he hung out with his friends on the street. He was living aimlessly, not thinking about what would happen years down the road. When his cousin was killed in a gang fight, Thomas realized that the life he was leading wasn't going to take him anywhere. He spoke to a military recruiter, because he knew he needed a change, but he wasn't ready to commit.

Then 9/11 happened. One of the largest upswings in enlistment occurred after that tragic event. Thomas, an African American, had been reading about the Tuskegee Airmen and felt proud of their dedicated service during World War II. They had saved over one hundred bombers. He wanted to do something positive with his life, and he thought maybe he could make a difference, too.

Thomas joined the army in February 2002 and turned nineteen in basic training at Fort Knox. There he specialized in operating heavy artillery, particularly Bradley tanks, which are fitted with heavy machine guns.

"My first deployment was in 2003, in Fallujah, Ramadi, and Tikrīt, by the Syrian border." Fatalities were high in most of the areas he served. Thomas remembers the death of his comrades, but he doesn't often discuss the details. It's not something he likes to relive. "It's in my head enough as it is," he says.

For his second deployment, he was stationed in Baghdad for a full year. His commanding officer wanted to send Thomas home for two months before he finished his tour. Iraq was brutal on the soldiers, and the commanding officers felt they needed time out of the country to recover. Thomas didn't want to go.

Thomas says, "I would rather stay because wrapping your mind around that scene twice in one year and having to get back into it all again is just too hard to do mentally. When you're home, you want to feel like being home, not on edge about having to go back—then you're never really at home."

The commanding officers were trying to protect men like Thomas, but he felt he knew himself better. Challenging an officer's judgment is not allowed in the army, though. When Thomas fought against his orders, he felt the commanding officers turned against him.

"We were still losing soldiers like crazy and it just got worse. The different groups, Sunnis and Shiites, were attacking each other at the end of 2005 into 2006. It was more dangerous at this time than any other."

On the ground, Thomas didn't know whether the locals were allies or enemies. Dangers were everywhere.

But one thing Thomas enjoyed was boxing, and he was good at it. He wanted to represent his unit in the All Army Boxing Championships, but his commander wouldn't sign the paperwork to allow Thomas to participate. Thomas thinks the refusal came because he'd challenged the order to go home. Thomas had pictured himself upholding the proud tradition of the Tuskegee Airmen, but instead he was growing disillusioned.

Despite these problems, Thomas and many of his fellow soldiers reenlisted. They didn't have the job skills for civilian life, and they figured the military was better than flipping burgers. But, Thomas says, many of these men were tired and burned out, while still facing constant threats to their lives. Private companies were sending over some of the body armor the men needed, but there was often not enough to go around. Men were risking their lives and dying, and Thomas felt the military wasn't doing all it could to protect them. He was just glad to make it home.

At Serenity Park, Thomas worked just as hard as Matt. He didn't talk much, and we didn't press him. He worked without question and never wanted to take his breaks. Matt noticed this, too. "I like this guy," he said.

"Let's get these aviaries clean," Matt would shout. He'd ask Thomas to help him haul bags of concrete and lumber. Matt and Thomas would unload tons of food from the delivery truck. Thomas spent hours scouring the grounds for branches and dragging them back; the parrots chewed the wood almost as quickly as he found it.

Matt was curious to see if his theory held. He watched to see which parrot Thomas would gravitate to and which parrot would gravitate toward him.

Matt guessed it would be Rainbow, a large male macaw. He really looked like a rainbow of a bird with a long, luxurious tail. His chest and much of his body were red, and his wings were accented with brilliant blues and greens. His wild cousins must have been magnificent, with their wings flashing in the sunlight as they flew over the green forests of South America. In spite of his dramatic good looks, he was a quiet bird. He didn't often call out for attention, instead watching the veterans surreptitiously as he preened or cracked open a nut. When he felt threatened, though, he struck out with his beak like a fist.

One day, Thomas went in to clean Rainbow's aviary.

Rainbow stood very still, watching Thomas carefully. He was rigid, feathers just a bit flared at the sight of this near stranger. As soon as Thomas shut the aviary door behind him, Rainbow lashed out, mouth agape. It looked as though he was going to strike with the full force of his powerful beak. At the last minute, though, he turned his head. Thomas jumped away but quickly laughed. "Nice fake uppercut, Rainbow. I know that move from boxing."

Thomas understood it was all about posturing. He had seen enough men on the streets and in the military putting on a tough act. Rainbow didn't want anyone to mess with him. He had to get a jab in to show he was tough. That didn't mean he actually wanted to hurt anyone.

Thomas started spending more time in the aviary. It wasn't long before Rainbow stopped threatening him. He'd learned that Thomas wasn't there to hurt him.

Thomas never did tell me or Matt more details about what he'd seen in his service. But he spent time talking to Rainbow. Bird and man would be quiet when anyone approached. Thomas is still quiet—it's part of his nature—but he is no longer withdrawn. He laughs and jokes like any other veteran here, and he can match anyone for hard work. The improvements in him are obvious to all of the staff.

Thomas and Rainbow would take fake jabs at each other, but Thomas would be smiling and Rainbow's eyes would glitter. There was trust between man and bird, and trust was healing for both. When he first came to Serenity Park, Thomas couldn't work with people. He was shy and suspicious, ready to lash out. Rainbow allowed him, albeit slowly, to learn to trust. Once he learned to trust one living creature, he started to be able to trust his fellow men and women.

Thomas remains a valuable and loved member of our close-knit crew, and Rainbow is his wingman. When Rainbow rides on his shoulders as he goes about his aviary cleaning chores, Rainbow's crooked tail curls around Thomas's neck.

Thomas remembers the story of his difficult birth. He had come into this world struggling, but he had made it. He was going to make it again. "I am blessed twice in my life," he says.

THIRTEEN

Grand Opening

You must do the thing you think you cannot do.

—ELEANOR ROOSEVELT

Matt had graduated from New Directions. He was sober and managing the symptoms of PTSD. Now he had to start building a life.

He chose Ronald, a massive 320-pound, six-foot-six African American man, as his sponsor at Alcoholics Anonymous. Matt had played football as an undergraduate at the University of Cincinnati. Ronald had played as a tackle for Kentucky, one of the Cincinnati Bearcats' main rivals. But Matt's choice had nothing to do with football. Ronald respected AA axioms like "Principles before personalities" and "One day at a time." Matt knew Ronald was devoted to staying sober.

As one of the Twelve Steps of AA, an alcoholic must tell his story to his sponsor. When Matt started talking about his time playing football, Ronald stopped him. "When did you play?" he asked.

It turned out the two men had played each other. "Wait a minute," said Matt. "I got my bell rung by you." Matt had gone down hard during one of the last games of the season, and Ronald was the one who'd hit him. They had met on one tough field, and here they were meeting on another—the arena of recovery.

Ronald lived in South-Central Los Angeles and brought Matt to his AA Home Group. Matt liked it there, even though he was the only white guy, and he rented a room in that part of town after graduating from New Directions. Still, even though it meant commuting in Los Angeles traffic, he arrived at Serenity Park every day by 6 a.m. and stayed until dark.

"I'm going to set the schedules and help recruit more veterans," he said before long.

Soon he was training all of the veterans, coordinating with the various VA programs that provide services to our staff, overseeing construction, and bringing in more parrots. Each day, he seemed to find another task he could take over. Within the year, Matt was running the day-to-day operations of the sanctuary, supervising the veterans, and writing grants to provide more funding for operations.

It felt good to know I had a working partner I could trust. Matt was the eldest child in his family and I was the youngest. Allowing him to take the role of someone I could depend upon felt natural. Besides, I had big dreams, and they wouldn't be realized if I couldn't share the responsibility.

"We need more aviaries," he said, and he found a way

to get it done. We needed more supplies, so he started a resource development team.

Once Matt became a manager, he raised enough money to triple the number of aviaries. We brought in more parrots and hired more veterans to care for them. Running and maintaining the sanctuary was expensive, and in addition we had to provide medical care for each bird. When Matt added up the costs and saw how much each new bird cost us, he convinced me to ask for an up-front donation from people surrendering their birds to help pay for their care. We weren't always able to collect the money, but when we could it was a tremendous help.

Even though I turned over many responsibilities to Matt, I still had to be at the sanctuary. There was always plenty of work for both of us. Besides, I didn't want to miss Sammy's welcoming "Hello are you" each day.

Around this time, I was completing my own psychoanalysis, and it gave me an awareness of my own mind that I had never had before. I had lived alone for much of my life, and I liked that. I had been self-sufficient. I'd dated. I had friends. But I'd also worn masks to please people and to keep them at a distance. I'd never taken the radical step of being vulnerable. Here I was, open at last, and I found myself talking to Matt.

Matt could tell when the veterans were struggling, when a bird was likely to attack, when someone needed a hug; he had remarkable emotional intelligence. He was the most sensitive macho man I had ever met. More than his good looks, I found his willingness and ability to be open and emotionally honest very appealing.

As I moved through my day, I found myself thinking, Wait until I tell this to Matt. When he had an appointment outside of the sanctuary, I started looking toward the entrance a few minutes before he was supposed to return.

He grew more protective of me. Once, I was leading a group of veterans on a tour. Matt was over by the aviaries and could hear what was going on. The guys were being loud. "Hey," Matt bellowed, "Dr. Lindner is talking. Everyone listen up."

They did. I could have managed on my own, but I appreciated him having my back.

I often caught Matt glancing at me. When an uncommunicative and physically imposing veteran spoke to me, I noticed Matt hovering nearby.

He smiled at me often. When one of our aggressive parrots finally allowed a veteran to stroke her feathers, Matt ran over to share his happiness with me.

I noticed, but notice was all I did. Even though I was never Matt's psychologist, I felt he was off-limits. I was still his boss (even though he was barely getting paid), and he had graduated from a program where I had been clinical director five years earlier.

I told myself that starting a relationship was a bad idea.

* * *

Serenity Park had been open for nearly two years, and we finally decided to have a grand opening. It was time for a celebration. Serenity Park was looking a lot more like a center for healing. When we began, we had just a few enclosures. Now we had a central entrance, and, to the right and left, two long rows of enclosures, each large enough for a couple of parrots to fly and a couple of humans to move around in comfortably. We had a small building with two kitchens, a quarantine area for sick birds, and room for storage. We had planted gardens and placed seating throughout our space.

But I also knew that a large event would get people thinking about us, and that meant potential new sources of funding—funding that our program always needed.

I wanted a large event, the kind that would get coverage in the media and spread the word about Serenity Park. I pictured musicians entertaining everyone, lights strung through the trees, a large tent with delicious food. People would dance and socialize and maybe pull out their checkbooks to help those beautiful parrots. We didn't have a party planner. We had to arrange everything from borrowing chairs and tables to purchasing Sterno for the chafing dishes. There were caterers, musicians, and celebrities to wrangle. We needed to get approval from many departments at the VA. We had to raise money.

I had experience planning events. When I first got licensed, not long after Hiro returned to Japan, I'd started a singles group for psychologists and psychiatrists: Psych Psingles. At one point, I had over seven hundred participating mental health professionals. I wanted to help my colleagues, but I also wanted to find someone, preferably someone emotionally expressive, for myself. It wasn't the time then, though. I just wasn't ready.

I organized cocktail parties, dances, conferences, and dinner shows. I coordinated it all: writing and mailing the invitations, buying the food and supplies, keeping guest lists, and dealing with all the small disasters that come with entertaining. It was a great deal of fun for several years, and thirteen couples got married because of Psych Psingles.

While putting together a party was something I could do, I'd never been this busy while organizing an event before. Hundreds of people were expected. Matt helped with the planning. When I was ready to scream because I had too many things going on at once, Matt would be there. "Let me handle this," he'd say. "You take care of what you need to do."

I watched him standing there, calm and strong while chaos swirled around him. He'd be smiling at me, shooing me away. That smile was nice.

I leaned on him, but it was just a friendship, I told myself. Once again, I'd go through the list of the many reasons he and I couldn't be together.

Matt and I both would spend time with the birds each day, even when things were at the most hectic. Our contact with the animals kept us both calm and grounded. When we were frazzled, when we wondered if all the moving parts would ever come together, when we dropped invitations in the mail even though we had the sickening feeling things would not work out as planned, there the birds were.

The birds were calm, in the moment, living day to day. They helped us take a breath. We'd make eye contact and smile when the birds climbed over to say hello. I understood how the birds worked with the veterans because I'd feel the tension melt from my shoulders when I talked to them. Matt cradled Ruby and relaxed. Sammy would let me pet her, and peace would wash over me. "Our" birds would sit, grooming, exploring, and cracking seeds. They would bob up and down, welcoming us. It put everything in perspective.

"Enjoy yourselves in this moment," they seemed to say; "the future is going to happen no matter what you do." We took that moment to connect to them and be together. Serenity Park worked its magic, and we realized that we were going to be fine.

While Serenity Park was opening up, so was I. My belief had always been that women and men do not need marriage to prove a lifetime commitment to their partners. But I was starting to realize, at some level, that Matt was part of my life. I needed him, not because a woman needs a man, but because I needed this particular man. We complemented each other. Still, I resisted.

One day, we received a check for a large donation. We drove to the bank together, and when we parked, our hands touched on the gearshift. "Lorin," Matt said, "I want to be with you."

My throat tightened. I looked at this strong man, a whirlwind of energy with a beautiful mind and heart.

"Your friendship is important to me, Matt. I care about you. Can we leave it at that?"

He respected my feelings, but he wasn't about to give up. As we worked to make the grand opening a reality, I started to question myself. I thought of Matt every night, but I convinced myself that I was making the correct decision.

"You should start dating," I said to Matt.

Matt froze. "Don't try to pawn me off on other women," he said, walking away. I'd never seen Matt angry with me before. Or perhaps it wasn't anger. It might have been hurt and frustration.

I wanted to go after him. But that was the wrong thing to do. I let him go.

Maybe Matt was right, I thought. Maybe I was pawning him off so I wouldn't have to think about him. I was taking the easy way out. Or maybe I wanted a better life for Matt. I knew he was special. I knew he needed to reconnect with life. I just didn't think that life should include being involved romantically with me.

Somehow, we worked our way through the dozens of crises that happen when you plan a big event, and it was time for Serenity Park's grand opening.

Mark Bittner, author of *The Wild Parrots of Telegraph Hill: A Love Story . . . with Wings*, was the keynote speaker. I had also invited the VA brass, including the West Los Angeles director and the director of the California Department of Veterans Affairs. My local Congress members, state senators, and the LA mayor's office sent aides with proclamations honoring the opening of a facility "to help veterans and parrots alike, suffering from problems with a common source— stress-related trauma." The current head of the West Los Angeles VA spoke, as did the clinicians in the programs who sent their veterans to work or volunteer at Serenity Park. The New Directions Choir sang, complete with a version of "Wind beneath My Wings" in my honor, and there was an opening chant by the local Chumash tribe. Robby Krieger, formerly of the Doors, sang at a pre-ceremony gathering. Loretta Swit, an actress best known for her work on *M*A*S*H*, donated some lovely paintings of macaws she'd made herself.

My oldest, best friends were at the grand opening. They couldn't help noticing the guy who seemed to be everywhere. "Are you interested in him?" one asked.

"We're trying to be just friends," I answered.

This friend spent much of the evening with Matt. She was flirting. She was a beautiful woman. Matt was flirting back.

How could he flirt with someone right in front of me? I had no right to be angry, I thought, but I was. He spoke with this woman at length, but when he noticed I needed him for something, he was there by my side.

I felt I should be honest with him; that's how he had been with me these last many months. "Matt," I said, "it bothered me to see you flirting."

"Lorin," he said, "if it matters to you, I'll never do it again."

He didn't even ask anything in return. He didn't tell me to stop dating other men. He was protective, but not jealous.

After the opening, I took a short trip to Utah. Bryce Canyon is one of my favorite places on earth, magical in its grandeur. I spent my days hiking, but every night I called Matt. I told myself that it was to check up on work at the sanctuary.

I realized I was being dishonest with myself. I knew that Bryce Canyon would have been even more magical with someone special to share it with.

I started asking Matt questions about his plans for the future; I knew what mine were. I wanted to expand my work with animals and start rescuing horses. I wanted to finally make my move to the country.

"So what do you think of living in the mountains, away from Los Angeles?" I asked.

"That's not a problem at all. I'll just get a helicopter so I can take care of the birds every day," Matt said. He was joking, but, knowing him, he probably would have found a way to make that happen.

"Lorin," Matt said, "I've told you how much I care for you. I still mean it."

"I care for you, too," I said.

"It's more than that. It's been more since I first saw you. I want to put my arms around you."

"You know I've been pushing you away," I said.

"I don't blame you." I could hear the smile in his voice; he felt he was gaining ground.

"Should we give it a chance?" I asked.

"I've wanted that since we met."

"I really do care about you, Matt."

"I love you, Lorin."

It is hard to remember why I had ever fought this.

FOURTEEN

Building a Flock

There are two ways of exerting one's strength:
one is pushing down, the other is pulling up.

—Booker T. Washington

We didn't have the budget to pay Matt to be a full-time manager. That didn't mean he wasn't a full-time manager. He was. It just meant he wasn't paid for his work. He couldn't afford to stay in Los Angeles.

Al Jacobson, my old friend who'd founded Garden of Eatin', had been diagnosed with Alzheimer's, and he came to me for help. He was in his nineties, and he had no close family. I sold my condo and moved in with my old friend. After all he'd done for me, it felt right. He was family. I helped with his finances, got him an accountant who was trustworthy, and kept away those who took advantage of him. I also oversaw his medical care.

Al could use another live-in caregiver. Matt needed a place to stay. It was a perfect trade. If Matt moved in with

Al, it could help me, too, since I struggled to work at the sanctuary and care for Al. As we finalized this arrangement, it felt as if we were adding to each other's lives in significant and productive ways.

I was worried about sharing a home with Matt. I shouldn't have been. We didn't squabble over little things. We made room for one another and respected each other. Matt, Al, and I celebrated Thanksgiving together (with Matt's first Tofurkey meal). It felt like being home. Not the homes from our childhood, but a better home that we'd built together.

We lost Al six months later, but I knew he was happy until the end. I would miss him terribly, but at least he'd spent the last moments of his life surrounded by love. He'd had ninety-four years, most of them healthy and active. Matt designed his headstone. It simply said: "Blue Corn Chips, Who Knew?" I think Al would have loved it.

We were a family. In case there was any doubt, we adopted three German shepherds from the local rescue center, something I had wanted to do for years but couldn't imagine doing in the city. We looked for that place in the country not too far from Serenity Park and found a perfect piece of land for horses in the mountains just north of Los Angeles. It was a mixture of wooded hills and scrubby lowland. We had to travel far down dusty, unpaved roads before we saw any neighbors. Jackrabbits ran through the fields and deer grazed quietly, darting away only when a human got too close. It already had a barn and an aviary. What more could I want? I barely even looked at the house. I knew Matt would make it a home.

Matt and I might correct each other sometimes, but we never belittle each other. I helped him give up smoking and meat. He helped me to break down my barriers to find true intimacy with a man. He taught me that we could do more as a team than we could working separately. We don't compete; we work to make each other's dreams happen. There's a current country-and-western song in which a woman cuts out pictures in a magazine, and then her husband makes those dreams come true. If I have a dream, it becomes Matt's as well.

I'd never believed in marriage, but Matt did. We were shopping at Costco one afternoon. He told me he was going to grab something. Moments later, I heard his voice over the loudspeaker. He was proposing. Matt always has to go big when he does things. The customers started applauding as he got down on one knee and handed me a ring. I kissed him and gave an emphatic yes.

"Wait," I asked. "This ring doesn't have a blood diamond, does it?"

Matt wrinkled his forehead. "Blood diamond?"

"A blood diamond. One that comes from a war zone. Mined with forced labor."

Matt groaned and hung his head. "That's one of the reasons I love you," he said, laughing. "You're always teaching me something."

He looked down at the ring. "And you're the only person I know who would answer a marriage proposal with a research project."

He made sure the diamond was conflict-free. I was proud to wear it, and I was proud to be with a man who honored the things I cared about.

Matt and I were married in June 2009 at Serenity Park, the place where we'd met, surrounded by the parrots and

veterans we both loved. It was a brilliantly clear Los Angeles day. There were fruits and flowers everywhere from our
friends who operated the local farmers market. Sammy was
there as the flower girl, and all the feathers I had collected
from her and Mango for the past twenty-two years were
turned into a beautiful bouquet. Ruby attended as well. Matt
looked so handsome in his tuxedo coat paired with black
shorts and Keds. I, too, dressed simply in a long, lightweight
white dress. Flowers—and that blood-free diamond—were
my only jewelry. A vegan caterer made a huge spread including a dark-chocolate fountain and triple-tiered calla
lily cake.

One of my biggest joys was having friends be part of
the ceremony. Dana Lyons, an environmental troubadour,
played songs from his album *At Night They Howl at the
Moon*, one of my all-time favorites. The New Directions
Choir director sang, as did our friends the Angels of Venice,
a group of three talented female musicians and vocalists.
Stilt Circus and a Brazilian calypso duo performed. And
our officiant, James Cromwell, a man who loves animals
and the environment and was the actor who played the
farmer in *Babe*, celebrated the occasion with a reading
that combined the wisdom of the songwriter Don Henley
with the poet Oriah Mountain Dreamer. It said in part,
"I don't care what you do for a living. . . . I don't care
what kind of car you drive" . . . "I want to know if you
will stand at the center of the fire with me and not shrink
back."

That was how I pictured Matt, the epitome of never
backing down, never backing away. That is how he lives each
and every day. And knowing this made this celebration one

of true meaning for me. It was a celebration of our lives, separate yet blending in joy, light, and love.

* * *

I knew Sammy had found peace as well. When I tell the story of Sammy at Serenity Park, it's a far different story than the dreadful morning of her capture.

This is what I see: Sammy opens her eyes to the gentle morning light filtering through the trees. Around her, she hears the calls of her flock, already awake and greeting the morning. She knows each bird by sound, all six dozen of them. Some she can see, and some she knows only by their voices. There are parrots of all colors, shapes, and sizes: macaws, African greys, conures, Amazons, cockatoos. These birds would never be found together in nature, but here they've become a family of sorts. She doesn't understand exactly what some of them are saying, but she's familiar with the sounds. They are comforting, expected.

Not long after the sun rises, the men and women arrive. Sammy knows them as well. One stops by her cage. "Hey, pretty girl, good morning." Sammy calls back: "Hello." She seems to know how people greet one another.

A woman comes into her aviary, and Sammy hops onto her shoulder. Most mornings, this person comes to see her, and she always pets her softly. Sammy's back itches, and the woman always seems to know exactly where to scratch. She's good at getting the sheaths off of Sammy's new feathers.

Sammy has learned that the people here will not grab her. There are no harsh yells, no cigarette smoke choking her breath. She knows she can trust their touch to be gentle.

A man brings in a tray with fresh blackberries, apple,

slices, and walnuts. Sammy hops off the woman's shoulders and onto the tray. She takes a bite of berry and throws the rest to the ground. She might come back later. There's always plenty to eat, and Sammy doesn't have to fear hunger. She'll take her time.

She hops around her aviary. Sometimes there's a nut hidden in the log under her perch. Nothing today. Then, in a corner behind a toy, she spots it. An uncracked pecan. Eureka. She scampers down and grabs it, then she carries her prize back up to her perch. She holds the nut in one foot while she cracks it with her beak. Then she pulls off stray bits of shell and tastes the nutmeat inside. Things always seem to taste better when you find them yourself.

Sammy watches as the people clean the aviaries around her. Some of her flockmates come to the people for attention. Others shout in warning for them to stay away. One always swoops for their heads; the men and women have learned to ring a bell to distract her before they go into that enclosure. Whether they welcome people or not, all the birds get the same attention and the same care.

Later, Sammy will search out more nuts hidden in her aviary. She'll groom her feathers. She'll climb and explore. There's always something new for her to search out.

It isn't the rainforest. Sammy will never live the life of a wild parrot. But she's comfortable here. She's found a way home.

* * *

Matt and I were not the only pair who mated for life.

Pilot, the Moluccan cockatoo who had helped Smitty go from shaking with withdrawal to reuniting with his family, was recovered enough to have a mate of his own. We placed our Moluccan cockatoo females—first Peanut, then Molly—next to Pilot. For days he did not go over to where they stood on the other side of the cage bars. He acted as if they didn't exist.

Then one day an owner brought in Kiwi, a beautiful snow-white umbrella cockatoo. The woman's husband had been diagnosed with Parkinson's disease, and it was progressing quickly. They could not afford live-in help, so it was up to her to do the caregiving. There would be no time for Kiwi. The woman didn't want to give up her companion, but she didn't want to neglect Kiwi either. "I've had her twenty-two years," she said, her voice trembling. "I don't know how I am going to live without her. I just know this is the right thing to do."

I reassured her that she could come see her bird whenever she liked, and knowing this helped her let go. She told me about Kiwi's life, how she'd been playful, loving, and always a little vain. When she first got Kiwi, she also had a Moluccan cockatoo, a male whom Kiwi was very attached to. He died unexpectedly and she never got another bird. Kiwi had been without parrot companionship for twenty years.

I watched Kiwi preen on her perch; she was in fine feather and seemed to know it. Maybe, I thought, I could try her with Pilot. I put her in the aviary next to his, and their bond was like magic. Even though they are different species, Kiwi and Pilot loved each other at once. They cooed to each other between the wire of the two aviaries. Pilot began gathering the tree stumps, branches, and ropes we leave out for the birds to chew in order to build Kiwi a nest. After a while, we put the birds together in a separate, neutral aviary to avoid territoriality and watched them closely, as Moloccan males can be aggressive. But Pilot and Kiwi shared a perch, grooming each other and softly "talking." It didn't take long to realize that they were safe, and content, together.

When Kiwi's owner returned to visit, Kiwi would not come down from her perch to see her. Kiwi and Pilot rarely moved more than a few feet from each other. The woman cried, not because she was upset that Kiwi was rejecting her, but because she realized that for twenty years Kiwi had missed that Moluccan cockatoo. Now she had another companion, and her owner was crying tears of joy.

* * *

Some birds bond only with other birds, some only with humans, and some with both. Sammy had shown interest in other birds at Earth Angel, and had even spent time in her enclosure with a few favorites, but she hadn't found a mate. I was beginning to think she would never bond with anyone but me. It made me sad.

I think finally being in a fulfilling marriage myself made me realize how much Sammy was missing. There are plenty of unhappy marriages in the world—as a psychologist I see more than most people do—and a bad marriage can tear two people down. A good marriage is different. It can make us stronger; the whole is greater than the sum of its parts. Still, humans can survive happily with no permanent partner. It's in a parrot's nature to want a mate.

Then Sammy met Little Girl and everything changed.

Little Girl was a Moluccan cockatoo, and with her pink-tinged feathers and bright crest, she looked a lot like Sammy.

Unlike Sammy, she still had most of her feathers. She had spent years in a garage, usually with the door down. In that unventilated space, most of Little Girl's days were dark and stifling. She didn't have people or birds to interact with.

Her owner came out to the garage occasionally to give Little Girl food or clean her cage, but most of the time she sat alone. She didn't even have a window to watch the outside world. She truly was in solitary confinement.

The neighbors heard Little Girl's cries, and they called the police. The police visited, but there was little they could do. There aren't laws protecting lonely parrots. The most they could do was cite the owner for the noise, and they didn't even do that.

The neighbors kept complaining, though, trying to get something done for the bird. Eventually, the owner called us. She was tired of dealing with the neighbors.

When we came to pick up Little Girl, the owner wasn't there to say goodbye. She said she was busy and left her son to open the garage for us. She'd said on the phone before we arranged the pickup: "If she wasn't so noisy I wouldn't have put her in there."

We took Little Girl out of the garage and drove her to our veterinarian. Once he cleared her for Serenity Park, it was time to find her a perch.

We decided to place Little Girl with Sammy. Sammy was never aggressive with Mango; she just wasn't crazy about him. Maybe a different bird would work. Sammy hadn't been interested in any males, so maybe it was time to test her with a female. I've observed several parrots through the years who, like some humans, prefer their own gender. Somehow, Matt and I both felt it was a good match.

We introduced the two birds slowly. First, we let them see each other for a while. Then, when they seemed comfortable, we put them on opposite ends of the enclosure. We let the birds take their time approaching one another. For Sammy and Little Girl, comfort seemed to come right away. Once we introduced them, they didn't have time for any of the other birds. The two groomed each other. They shared a perch. They seemed to talk together in a language that was their own. They were physically affectionate. Little Girl had suffered for a long time, but she was no longer alone.

Sammy was enthralled by Little Girl. She still got excited when I came to visit, and she still let me cuddle her, but she'd soon move back to Little Girl's side. Sammy had been the first bird I'd been close to and I missed our special interactions, but I was thrilled for both of them.

We had both found our mates. Everything was as it should be.

FIFTEEN

Warriors and Wolves

Motivation is when your dreams put on work
clothes.

—Benjamin Franklin

If this were just a love story, I'd end it here. But joining my
life with Matt's meant we could combine our skills to save
more animals.

Matt helped me fulfill my visions. I wanted to rescue
horses, but we would need the proper enclosures before we
brought any animals to our new home. There had recently
been a fire in the area, and there were many downed trees
that had yet to be removed by the Forest Service. "Two birds,
same food," Matt said with a wink. Matt went out with his
truck and trailer and hauled in over two thousand logs. He
brought them back and threw himself, body and mind, into
building those enclosures. We loved the idea of reusing the
wood and buying recycled chain-link fencing. We wanted to
help animals without consuming more resources.

As the fences got closer to completion, I thought about which horses to rescue. I had known for many years that pharmaceutical companies use pregnant mares to manufacture drugs for hormone-replacement therapy. Pregnant mares are packed together as if they're on an assembly line and catheterized to collect their urine. When the horses give birth, drug manufacturers get rid of the males, who are of no use to them. Some friends in the animal rescue movement were inspecting a factory, and they found a male colt literally thrown into the trash, still alive. He was weak and entirely alone.

We took him in: he was our first Premarin (a drug name that literally stands for "pregnant mare urine") rescue. The second was a "downed mare," a horse who could no longer stand up on the assembly line. Only four years old, she was pregnant for the second time, and she was severely underweight. We named her Tara, after the plantation in *Gone with the Wind*, because when I saw her I pictured Scarlett O'Hara kneeling over the barren fields, swearing: "I'll never go hungry again."

Her baby, Tie Dye, is a little filly. She will never suffer as her mother did, pregnant and catheterized, on an assembly line. She rustles through my pockets with her dexterous lips to find remnants of horsie cookies. People ask us if we plan to ride her and we immediately respond in unison, "No!" She's free to live her life as she wants, and we can't imagine her wanting us on her back. I can picture her turning around and looking at a rider as if to say, "What the heck are you doing back there?" Needless to say, she's very spoiled.

Not far from our home in the mountains, there is a big rescue facility where horses are allowed to roam. We went to visit because they care for former racehorses who have been abandoned, and I thought one might be a good companion for the horses we'd taken in. They also had something unexpected: a wolfdog. We had never seen one before and asked if he was up for adoption.

"He's part wolf: you'd need all kinds of permits and secure containment," the facility manager said.

She explained that wolfdogs are a growing problem. Formerly they were known as wolf hybrids, but wolves and dogs are actually the same species, capable of reproducing and having fertile offspring. They've become fashionable pets, so breeders are turning them out as quickly as they can. Unlike domesticated dogs, however, they still have the traits that make wolves effective hunters and pack animals in the wild. They haven't been bred for thousands of years to live comfortably with humans, as dogs have. They rarely make good pets. The story was all too familiar to me from parrot rescues. People are buying wolfdogs because they find them fascinating, but they aren't prepared to care for a wild animal.

The problem of exotic-animal ownership was brought to most everyone's attention in 2011 when a man in Ohio let all of his rare Bengal tigers, African lions, leopards, grizzly bears, wolves, and monkeys out of their cages minutes before killing himself. Over fifty animals were killed by police and wildlife officers as a result. Ohio had some of the weakest prohibitions against keeping wild animals as pets. Not anymore. But what is worse are that thousands, perhaps millions, of exotic animals are still coming out of breeding facilities every year. Just as for the parrots, there are simply not enough good homes or sanctuaries for them all.

"Okay," I said, "I understand. We'll get whatever permits

are required. Just please keep us in mind if another one comes your way."

We contacted wolfdog rescue agencies and found out what we needed to do. An expert on secure containment visited our property and explained how to build the enclosures. Once we had our first enclosure built, he came back for an inspection. He approved it. We called the place that had the wolfdog to let the people there know we were ready.

It didn't take long before they called us back: "There is a wolfdog at the Bakersfield shelter who is going to be put to sleep by noon today. Get him if you can." I immediately called Matt, who was driving to Serenity Park, as he did nearly every day. It was in the opposite direction from the shelter. But this day Matt had a problem with his trailer's electrical system, and the only place that could help was in Bakersfield. It was perfect synchronicity. He was literally across the street from the shelter. Matt got there minutes before noon.

At the shelter, though, they claimed that the wolfdog was gone. Something told Matt they weren't telling him the truth. He walked into the back room. The dog was strapped down on a table and muzzled. His fur was coated with feces and urine. Shelter employees had been practicing placing IVs in him, and blood was everywhere.

"I'm taking this dog," said Matt. He took him out of the restraints and carried him to his truck. He came back to glare at them and threw the adoption fee down on the table. We had our first wolfdog. He was only about six months old and had been brought to the shelter because he growled when the owner's five-year-old lay on him while he was sleeping. The animal was just trying to tell the boy to back off, as he would with a younger pup in his pack, but for a parent the sound must have been terrifying. They gave their wolfdog away.

We named him Wiley because he looked like a little coyote. He bonded with Matt almost immediately, and the two became inseparable. Wiley was gentle with everyone. He didn't even bother the parrots at Serenity Park, so Matt was able to bring him to work every day.

The veterans loved Wiley. Matt believes that veterans and wolfdogs are natural together. Both can be predators. Both are misunderstood. Both are often abused and neglected. Both are pack animals. Matt says that when soldiers come back home they have a struggle inside of them, and they can't figure out how to stop being soldiers and start being citizens. We see a similar struggle in the wolfdogs. They want to sleep on the couch, but they also want to rip the books out of your bookcase. They're pack animals, so they don't like to be alone, but they're also wild. They don't easily take orders. Unlike domesticated dogs, they don't respond to aggression with submission. You need to learn to deal with certain wolfdogs as wild animals, not as pets.

Matt got the idea of creating a program similar to Serenity Park called Warriors and Wolves. We would have the veterans caring for the wolfdogs here at our property in the mountains, just as they care for the parrots. We were discovering that there are many wolfdogs in need of rescue. I told Matt, "Just put it out to the universe what you want and you will see how quickly it will come."

Soon we had ten wolfdogs, and Matt got busy building more enclosures. Nothing Matt does is small-scale. These enclosures are not cages; they are two-to-three-acre habitats, complete with underground dens. The fences are high, much higher than you'd find around a family home, and go far underground as well. Our enclosures are scattered over the hilly terrain. They're filled with trees and boulders. The wolfdogs have room to run, explore, and hide.

As with the parrots, there were more wolfdogs available than we could handle. People were buying wolfdogs from breeders with little understanding of what they were getting themselves, their families, and their neighbors into. The wolfdogs were jumping over their fences—even eight feet can be too low—or they were digging underneath their fences (wolfdogs are proficient diggers). They are excellent hunters and quite territorial. They were killing neighborhood cats and dogs.

To prevent escape, owners would keep their wolfdogs in crates or small cement dog runs, where they would howl all night. Like parrots and like us, wolfdogs are pack animals, and isolation is torture. Neighbors complain. Animal Services shows up. In many counties and states, it's illegal to keep wolfdogs. When a wolfdog ends up in a shelter, it's almost always euthanized immediately. They cannot be adopted, so why spend money on their care? Matt told people in the rescue community that he wanted to rescue pure white Arctic wolfdogs as well, and soon we had four.

I loved these animals, too, but wolves and wolfdogs need raw meat. I had spent most of my life fighting for animal rights. Unlike humans, who can happily and healthily live on a vegan diet, carnivores cannot survive on beans and grains. I had always wanted to rescue parrots and horses. Neither animal eats meat. I could help them without harming other animals. But wolfdogs were another matter.

Soon after the wolfdogs came to live with us, a calf with

deformities was born on a nearby farm. It would never have a normal life, and the farmer slaughtered it. The farmer offered the carcass to Matt, who butchered it for our wolfdogs. I knew that calf was going to die anyway, but I couldn't stand the thought that we had something to do with its death. "Never again," I said to Matt.

Matt honored that wish. He searched for a way to get meat without hurting any additional animals. He found Quest Recycling. Quest helps supermarkets divert waste from landfills. It takes food that would be thrown away by stores because it's approaching its sell-by date and finds places that can use it, including zoos and sanctuaries like ours. But Quest required Matt to pick up at least ten thousand pounds of food per week, not just meat but all the perishables the stores throw out, clearly more than our animals could use, so Matt began collecting on behalf of several sanctuaries. He felt it would be worth the effort if he could feed many more carnivores.

We don't harm animals. Instead, we're taking perfectly good meat that would go to a landfill if we didn't use it. In a way, it keeps those animals' lives from being wasted. And the wolfdogs get a variety of foods that we would never be able to afford, even if we were inclined to buy them: fresh salmon filets, roasts, beef liver. To this food we add supplements and even a few vegetables. They wouldn't be as healthy as they are if we fed them anything else.

* * *

I never quite pictured myself Dumpster diving, but I have to admit part of me loves it.

Working to reuse food waste is tough manual labor. One day in late July, we were inside Matthew's thirty-eight-foot trailer, a gift from animal lover Bob Barker's foundation—not exactly a Dumpster but close. We were sifting through a load that must have been at least twenty thousand pounds, and it all had to be sorted and distributed to other rescue groups. Matt woke up before dawn to drive this enormous trailer to the various supermarkets dispersing the food. It was unseasonably hot that day, and we needed to get it safely into the hands of animal rescuers, or disposed of, before it began to rot.

Warriors and Wolves is an official wolf sanctuary now, recognized by all the federal, state, and county agencies assigned to that task. With four dozen animals including wolves and wolfdogs, coyotes, foxes, and horses, we must set aside the food we'll need for the week and the produce we'll bring to Serenity Park. Most of the produce is perfectly good to feed to the birds: apples with brown spots, packages with one crushed berry, or cases of plums the stores just can't sell. I wouldn't feed anything to our animals that I wouldn't feel comfortable eating myself.

So there we were sorting. Food that is rotting or smells bad goes straight into our dump trailer. Most of it, though, is just overstocked inventory or produce with slight imperfections. The problems are only cosmetic, or easily solved with a paring knife, but customers won't buy it. Sell-by dates, many largely arbitrary, send perfectly good packaged food from the shelves to the landfill. Our country produces so much food that we're picky, and few people think about the waste that pickiness generates.

Matt was sweating; he had been hauling around barrels of food all day in heat over ninety degrees, and the dust from the windy summer day clung to his body. The amount of waste was bothering me; I was trying to think how we could use it all.

Matt sighed and rubbed the sweat off the back of his neck. "Lorin," he said, "I need you to decide what's going to the birds and what's staying here."

There was a package of plums, perfect except for one with a small bruise. There were sugar snap peas, still good, with a use-by date a week off. There were boxes of mangoes. They looked perfect, but there must have been some reason for rejecting them, probably no room on the shelves. "Can you believe this? So much waste," I said.

"Just put everything into piles. Tell me what you want."

"Do you think we could do something with this?" I said, pulling out a bunch of slightly wilted carrots. "Maybe for the horses."

"Lorin, I need you to focus."

I knew there'd been a crate of blackberries I wanted to give to the birds. "Did you see those blackberries anywhere?" I asked Matt.

He sighed and pointed to the right of the truck. "If it goes to the sanctuary, put it there. If it's going to the dump, put it in the barrel, and if it stays here, put it behind me."

There were a couple of tons of produce still on the truck.

"Sweetheart, I love you, you're wonderful, but if you don't decide where these things are going, I'm going to scream."

Matt rarely loses his patience with me so I simply said: "I love you, too."

I began going through the rest. I still don't know what happened to those blackberries.

* * *

Our lives are not perfect. It would be nice to know where the money to keep the sanctuaries running is going to come from.

It would be nice for Matt to draw a salary. I could use an extra fifty years to get all the things I want to do accomplished. There are losses and regrets. And, of course, Matt will probably always suffer from some symptoms of PTSD.

But our relationship is strong. Early in our marriage, we made a pledge we call the Paul and Linda McCartney Oath. They vowed never to sleep apart and never did in twenty-seven years except when Paul was in jail in Japan for nine days for marijuana possession. We hope to do the same, minus the jail time.

I am allowed to be exactly who I really am around Matt. That is truly the greatest gift we can give anyone. I hope I do the same for Matt; I know that is what I aspire to do. We're finding peace and healing one day at a time.

Serenity Park has over six dozen birds, and they're being cared for by veterans. We are now running Warriors and Wolves in two states. Combat veterans come out here and connect with pack animals like themselves. They grow and trust and heal. Nature is working its magic on bird, wolfdog, and man, and they're all working their own magic on each other.

Epilogue

Although Serenity Park is an idyllic place, I missed having my sweet cockatoo with me. Sammy and Mango had been my family, and I wanted Sammy near me. Once we moved to the country, I decided to bring Sammy and Little Girl to our home. This wasn't an isolated cage in a garage. They had their own room right off the living room. It had glass on three walls. They could see the surrounding countryside, and they could see us. They had every toy imaginable. We built them an elaborate stand, fifteen feet high with three levels, as a playpen. Sammy was a constant chewer, and I would bring her tree branches galore. She shared everything with Little Girl.

The two lived with us for seven years.

And then one evening when I returned home with Matt

from an excursion off the mountain, Sammy was standing on the ground. Not a good sign. Tree-dwelling birds rarely spend much time on the ground, because there are too many predators. Matt and I looked at each other and without a word wrapped her in a blanket and drove right back down the mountain to our trusted avian veterinarian, Dr. Attila Molnar.

As we drove, I thought about that horrible night when I took Mango, bleeding and dazed, from Ojai to the all-night veterinarian. This time was different. I had the support of my husband, who called Dr. Molnar to let him know when we would arrive and asked him to prepare the hospital for Sammy. Still, I had the same feeling of helplessness, of wishing I could just do something to make her better. It was midnight when we got there. I talked to Sammy in calming tones, but something was very distant about her. She didn't make eye contact. She stared ahead, focusing on nothing.

We sat with her all night, willing her to just stay awake. "Come on, sweetheart, just hold on," I urged.

There was little the veterinarian could do for her.

She closed her eyes. Her breath was shallow. I focused my energy on keeping her chest moving. For an instant, Sammy opened her eyes and locked them on mine. She used her beak to grab onto the side of the cage and extended her little foot out. I grasped her toes and she wrapped them around my finger, holding on tight. I willed myself to stand there for as long as she could hold on. It felt as if we shared the same pulse. As she slipped away I felt my heart skip a beat, and I had to gasp for breath. That's when she let go, and I knew she was gone.

Matt was standing right there and wrapped his arms

around me, and I was grateful not to have to suffer alone this time.

The veterinarian diagnosed lead poisoning. The onset of her illness was sudden, thankfully, but the lead might have been building up in her system for weeks. We fed her a natural diet, we didn't use harsh chemicals near her, and we made sure all her toys were safe. What could have poisoned her? There was a single, old cabinet near the ceiling of her room. Maybe it had lead paint. But Sammy never flew. How had she gotten up there?

I felt as if I'd failed her. This was Sammy, the one animal, more than any other, who'd inspired me to do the work I was doing. I had never met another cockatoo like her. I had never invested this much of my life in any one being. We had shared twenty-eight years together. We really do invest our heart and soul in our loved ones, and we lose a little piece of ourselves when they are gone.

Except it didn't feel like a little piece at the time. It felt as if I'd lost an enormous part of myself I could never get back.

Little Girl went back to Serenity Park, and, after a period of mourning, she began to bond with Casper, an umbrella cockatoo surrendered by her senior owner. This owner, thankfully, provided financially for her bird, and she still visits her little "love bug." It's some consolation to see Little Girl and Casper beginning to groom one another and to see them taking the first steps toward building a life together.

I could also console myself with the fact that at least Sammy had helped heal more souls than most parrots, or even humans, ever could. I'll always be grateful that Sammy entered my life. I can still hear her cries echoing through the dark streets of Beverly Hills. That cry rescued me. It

Mango on my arm; Sammy on Tippi Hedren's arm.

Acknowledgments

When I first heard a professor talk about how he dedicates his books to his students, I wondered why. Of course, I have long since realized the reason for that. We learn so much from our students that it is an often unacknowledged interchange. Our patients offer a similar gift. I wouldn't have known about the missing pieces of treatment, the places that weren't being reached by medications and traditional Western-based psychotherapies, had it not been for some of the men and women veterans who were willing to open their minds and ultimately their hearts to me.

I must thank the VA Greater Los Angeles Healthcare System. So many clinicians and other staff I have met only have the veterans' best interests at heart and devote themselves daily to that end. John Keaveney, Charles Dorman, and Ida Cousino helped start me on that path, and people like Earl Gardner, Leslie Martin, and Larry Williams keep that work going every day. There are too many others to name, and thankfully so.

I also am grateful to all the bird lovers who do right by parrots and to those parrots I have had the opportunity to care for and whose ways I have learned. Parrots like Sammy and Mango, of course, but also Julius, Little Girl, Casper, Ruby, Maggie, Joey, Dandy, Pilot, Rainbow, Sid, and Stevie. They have taught me what they need to thrive in this foreign land. And helping them thrive are veterans like Lilly, Thomas, Smitty, Jody, Barry, Mary Ellen, Jonathon, Steven, and Duke. Thank you for sharing your stories. A big shout-out must go to Liz, our nonveteran go-to person.

No book writes itself, and without expert support and counsel there are many manuscripts that never see the light of day. Therefore, I offer a heart filled with gratitude to Elisabeth Dyssegaard at St. Martin's Press, who handpicked this book and molded it to fruition with insight, kindness, and laser precision. Elisabeth had learned about the work being done at Serenity Park Sanctuary after reading the original beautifully crafted *New York Times Magazine* article by Charles Siebert. Elisabeth and Peter McGuigan of Foundry Media then encouraged me to tell this story, and with the help of the skilled and patient staff at St. Martin's it took flight. I thank them all for their astute guidance. Elizabeth Butler-Witter took my overly scientific writing and made my story more palatable for you, the reader. Not an easy effort, and I am grateful.

I have to thank my brother and sister, who always took care of their baby sister in the gentlest, most caring ways possible, with a little ribbing on the side. Their love of animals started it all. Most of all, I need to thank my husband, whose love, kindness, wild wit, and unprecedented hard work and dedication act like a pillar of support for me and all of the animals. Always standing at the center of the fire with me. You truly are my twin flame and flockmate.